MARKETS
OF PARIS

Markets of Paris

DIXON AND RUTHANNE LONG

PHOTOGRAPHS BY ALISON HARRIS

THE LITTLE BOOKROOM

NEW YORK

Book design: Louise Fili Ltd

Printed in China

Second Printing

Library of Congress Cataloging-in-Publication Data

Long, Dixon.
Markets of Paris / by Dixon and Ruthanne Long.
p. cm.
Includes bibliographical references and index.
ISBN-13: 978-1-892145-45-1 (alk. paper)
ISBN-10: 1-892145-45-6 (alk. paper)
1. Markets–France–Paris–Guidebooks. 2. Paris (France)–
Guidebooks. I. Long, Ruthanne. II. Title.
HF5474.F9P34 2006
381'.180944361–dc22   2006020978

Published by The Little Bookroom
1755 Broadway, 5th floor, New York, NY 10019
(212) 293-1643 Fax (212) 333-5374
editorial@littlebookroom.com   www.littlebookroom.com

Distributed by Random House
and in the UK and Ireland by Signature Book Services

For Ruthanne, who always believed in this book

Fluctuat nec mergitur

CONTENTS

Introduction

WE HAVE A LOVE AFFAIR WITH MARKETS. IT BEGAN WHEN WE LIVED IN PARIS IN THE 1960S, AND THE FLEA MARKETS were the best places to find inexpensive furniture and household goods. Later, the open-air food markets transformed that affair into a marriage. The abundance of good things to cook and to eat, their freshness, and the good will of the vendors gathered us in an embrace that never let us go.

After writing *Markets of Provence* we realized that others shared our feelings about markets. We talked with friends, and the idea emerged of a book about the markets of Paris. But it was not to be a book only about open-air food markets. For one thing, Americans visiting Paris more often stay in a hotel than in a rented house or apartment, and their needs are different. And for another, our foray into the subject showed us how many different and exciting markets there are that sell items other than food.

What is the magic of markets? Above all, it's the opportunity to observe a social experience that is quintessentially French and independent of class. In the markets, real people fill real needs for food, clothing, tools, household goods—sustenance for the body—but also search for books, stamps, letters, and historical artifacts that nurture the mind and the soul.

Moreover, there's no requirement that the observer participate (though you may strike up a conversation or two). In a market, you're plunged into an authentic experience in which you can be as anonymous as you wish, or speak up to anyone you happen to rub elbows with.

Markets are places where shoppers seek (and find) the best prices for the goods they are buying. As we define it, a market is a place where you can find a lot of the same thing at attractive prices. When—and if—you feel like spending some money, you can be confident that the price will be competitive.

There is a market in Paris for fabrics, and another for old paper goods. Birds and small animals have markets of their own. Similar kinds of shops have migrated to common locations that function as markets for antiques, ceramics, fine art, textiles, musical instruments, overstocked designer clothing and just about anything else imaginable.

As for open-air food markets, there are more than sixty, each in a different location in the city and open two or three times a week all year long. Add to this thirteen covered food markets and a dozen pedestrian streets where stalls push out on the sidewalk, extending the reach of commerce.

Crisscrossing the city by foot and Métro, we visited markets for stamps and phone cards, prints, leather, and used books. We already knew about the Clignancourt flea market, but we stumbled on the *brocante* (bric-a-brac) market near the Porte de Vanves, and the market for clothing, tools, and electric appliances at the Porte de Montreuil.

Over the course of many visits we became familiar with the geography of Paris. The deeper we dug, the more there was to learn. When we go back we embrace the city as an old friend whose habits and idiosyncrasies we recognize. But it's a friend who is constantly growing and changing, and who can still surprise and inspire us.

How to use this book

THE MARKETS ARE A GREAT WAY TO SEE PARIS WITH FRESH
EYES AND TO MEET THE PEOPLE UP CLOSE. THIS BOOK
will take you into parts of the city where you may never have been, and
show you markets whose existence you might never have guessed.

We've grouped markets in six geographic areas. The selection of our
favorite markets within those areas—those that we've chosen to describe
at length—is based on several reasons: most are bustling and colorful
(such as rue d'Aligre); some are located in places that are interesting for
cultural reasons (such as Saxe-Breteuil in the elegant 7th arrondissement,
and Barbès in the predominantly North African part of the city). Each of
these markets offers goods at competitive prices, attracting an active local
clientele.

At the end of each section there is a list of every market we visited
with a brief description of each. Sidebars in each section identify related
places or facts of interest. In addition, we suggest some possible itineraries, organized by days of the week. Finally, we provide a list of restaurants we like, and a short bibliography.

*Here are some practical suggestions for making your visits to markets easy,
enjoyable, and productive:*

✦ Always take a map. We like *Paris pratique par arrondissement*, published by l'Indispensable. You can find it in the magazine stands in train

stations and in bookstores like FNAC, both as a 96-page pocket book and as a foldout map.

✦ We get around Paris by Métro and on foot, using taxis if the weather turns rainy or our feet falter. Friends use the bus, but we find the subway quicker and easier. We usually buy a *carnet* (a book of ten tickets costing €10.70), because ticket booths are often inexplicably closed and there may be long lines at the machines. For visits longer than a few days, look into the electronic passes available at most Métro stations.

✦ Automated teller machines (ATMs) are generally found inside or near the entrances of banks. Money changers in small street booths give good service at competitive rates. Upscale shops, and some vendors in the larger markets, will take credit cards. Most will take a check in euros on a French bank account.

✦ Business hours are not as firm in Paris as in large American cities. The government sets opening and closing hours for food markets, but you will rarely find much to buy before 8 am, and the stands start to close up by 1 or 1:30 pm. Shops generally open at 10 or 11 am and stay open until 6 or 7 pm, but they may close for lunch from noon until 2 pm or later. Galleries and antique shops may open only three or four days a week, from late morning or afternoon to early evening.

✦ In most shops and galleries, travelers can ask that the French value-added tax, or VAT of about 20 percent, be reimbursed if you spend more than €175 in one place. This requires some paperwork, but it's not onerous. You may have to wait in line at the airport for Customs approval. However, for purchases of this amount or more, it may be worth the effort.

✦ We're often asked if we bargain: yes, but it helps to be comfortable in French (unless the salesperson speaks English). Prices in food markets are not negotiable, though vendors often lower them dramatically in the last thirty minutes to clear their stands. If you're not sure what price you can get, there's a simple and polite way to ask: *"C'est le meilleur prix?"* Is that your best price?

✦ Some shops will ship heavy or bulky items for you. If you need your purchase quickly you'll want it shipped by air. But if you can wait a few months, it can go by sea—the preferable method if you're buying an armoire or chest of drawers.

The question of opening and closing hours of the markets is complex and can be confusing. The hours provided here come from an official publication of the City of Paris, but there may be differences by season, and by arrondissement, each of which has its own City Hall. In general, it's safe to assume that an open-air market will be open by 8 am and will close at or shortly after 1 pm, even when published times are earlier or later. Covered markets observe schedules typical of food shops—open in the morning, closed for lunch, and open again from late afternoon until early evening.

The book is designed to go with you to Paris. We've kept our presentations brief and identified people and places that caught our interest. But you'll make your own discoveries. Whatever your interest or the length of your stay, you'll find a market to fascinate and reward you. So, *bon voyage*, and be sure to visit the markets the next time you see Paris, and the next, and the next...

PARIS CENTER-RIGHT BANK

1st, 2nd, 3rd, and 4th arrondissements
Le Louvre, les Halles, l'Île de la Cité

MARKETPLACES

Marché aux Fleurs et aux Oiseaux

FLOWER AND BIRD MARKETS

PLACE LOUIS LÉPINE, L'ÎLE DE LA CITÉ, 1ST ARR.

🚉 CITÉ

FLOWERS: MONDAY-SATURDAY 9 AM-6 PM

BIRDS: SUNDAY 8 AM-1 PM

EVERY DAY BUT SUNDAY, THE BIGGEST AND BEST FLOWER MARKET IN PARIS SPREADS OUT ON L'ÎLE DE LA CITÉ. TWO long green buildings that look like war relics house specialty shops for orchids, roses, bonsais, and every kind of potted houseplant, as well as fertilizer, seeds, books, and tools. In the adjacent quai de la Corse, fresh flowers are sold from open stalls by the stem or the bunch. This is the place to come if you want to brighten a rented apartment. But don't take flowers as a hostess present; she may think you suspect her of poor house-keeping. Chocolates are safer.

With the approach of November 1, the day of remembrance (called Toussaintes, or All Saints Day), you'll be staggered by the abundance of chrysanthemums, traditional for this holiday. In addition, varieties of bamboo, fig, and palm in every season are myriad; choysias, hemlocks, and heathers compound the blend and add to the delight. If you're in a hotel, you may yearn for the color or crave the perfume a bunch of freesias can give. Whatever the reason or season, a stroll through this extraordinary market is a delight to one's senses, a calm and refreshing stop amid the clamor and bustle of Paris.

You might take home from the stand opposite the Métro entrance some note cards or postcards on botanical themes. There are also beautiful little birdhouses made of white birch with thatched roofs (lightweight and very French). Farther along the same aisle are bamboo birdhouses. There are burlap totes with leather handles and corners, unusual garden tools, and a set of six beverage glasses in a wire tray for outdoor dining.

In the adjacent building, Au Jardin d'Edgar features miniature plants, including bonsai, for terraces and balconies. Take a look at La Maison d'Orchidée et Plantes Carnivores for something truly different. Claude Bouchard sells little dolls in historic costumes known as Santons de Provence and tea towels with regional prints, in case your trip doesn't include time in the south of France.

On Sunday, most of the flower shops are closed and the weekly bird market claims the long, open sheds. Perhaps not every bird imaginable as a pet can be found here, but you'll see all that thrive in the Parisian climate. The largest cages hold solemn gray parrots. Beside them are their green cousins, raucous as clowns, exploring their space, nudging and crowding each other on their perches like naughty boys. The market resonates with their trills and whistles, and occasionally a wild screech knifes through the air.

One brilliant Sunday morning we visited the bird market to gaze at the latest offerings. Established sellers were arrayed against the back of the sheds with their big birds, fat sacks of seed, and elaborate cages. Their merchandise is protected from wind and weather, and clients can be comfortable in all but the most inclement conditions. Along the sidewalk under the edge of the roof are tradesmen with stacks of small cages holding dazzling little multicolored finches and charming golden canaries.

You will also see equipment for raising and keeping birds: cages of every size and style, food, medicines, and books about the classification, care, and diseases of songbirds. Charming outdoor birdhouses are for sale (about €1.50), and in the same stall are as many as fifty kinds of bird-seed. A box of sawdust reveals a squirming mass of orange-colored meal worms, the tartare of the avian diet. What luck to be a caged bird in Paris!

Down the center of the market is the casual trade, people with a few nestlings or a single bird. There are scruffy interlopers here, too: a rough-looking fellow with a basin of goldfish and a box of turtles, a mys-terious Gypsy woman with a basket of puppies. In the spring, bunnies are displayed so that children can·stroke their fur and dream of taking one home.

Somehow, it all works without apparent conflict. Once in a while two gen-darmes in dark blue pants and light blue shirts stroll through the market, but they seem more interested in their own conversation than in policing any bad behavior on a sunny Sunday morning.

Louvre des Antiquaires

LOUVRE OF ANTIQUE DEALERS

2, PLACE PALAIS ROYALE, 1ST ARR.

🚊 PALAIS ROYAL-MUSÉE DU LOUVRE

TUESDAY-SUNDAY 10 AM-6 PM;

some shops open later and close from noon to 2 pm or later.

ENTER FROM PLACE DU PALAIS ROYAL, WITH ITS COLUMNS, TOPIARY, AND ORNATE CHANDELIER, OR THROUGH THE glass doors on rue de Marengo. Either way, you are in for a stunning experience. This massive, elegant structure was built in 1852 to house the department store Grand Magasin du Louvre. Some years ago it was renovated to provide space for a group of upscale antique shops.

Two hundred fifty shops on three floors are crammed with French decorative arts and furnishings from the Middle Ages to the twentieth century, and there is a rich collection of material from the Middle and Far East. Along with another group of shops on the left bank of the Seine, this is an important concentration of antiques. (For additional information about antique markets, see entries for Carré Rive Gauche des Antiquaires, Village Suisse des Antiquités, and Marché aux Puces de Clignancourt.)

Even if you buy nothing, the education is worth the cost of an hour or two wandering these aisles. On our last visit a display of medieval guns, armor, and instruments of torture on the ground floor transfixed us. Another window held a whole army of toy soldiers. Still another held a collection of French military medals and national awards. Upstairs, Laurence Jantzen had arrayed an immense diversity of canes, walking sticks, and riding crops, some of which might even fit in your suitcase.

Every shop has plate-glass windows and bright lighting. Many are small and their contents can be viewed comfortably from outside. But even if the door is closed and the owners are quietly eating a sandwich or drinking coffee in the back, your animated presence in front of the window can coax them out to answer a question. In any event, if something catches your fancy, don't hesitate to go in for a closer look.

Oil paintings are beautifully lighted and appear important even if the artist has been forgotten for a century or more. There is a good bit of rococo sculpture and a plethora of decorative objects for your living

room or library. At the basement level, you'll find antique silver and estate jewelry, things easily transported though they may not be within your budget.

A small café-bar on the second floor serves drinks and sandwiches, and there are comfortable places to rest. There is no more mesmerizing place in Paris to stroll and, as the French say, *lécher les vitrines*— lick the shop-windows—even better if you're a serious buyer with money to spend.

Hôtel Drouot Richelieu

TO EXPLORE THE FULL RANGE OF THE MARKET EXPERIENCE IN PARIS, WE VISITED THE DROUOT AUCTION HOUSE AT THE corner of rue Drouot and rue Rossini, its location since 1852. While the neighborhood has become a bit seamy, the auction house survives, like an elderly gentleman living in a deteriorating environment. Auctions are open to the public, and auction information is published in *PariScope*, a magazine available for €0.40 at news kiosks (a new issue comes out every Wednesday).

The building itself seems to us an architectural hodgepodge; bands of gray and black marble on the floor and walls of the entrance level are a bit depressing, and the exterior treatment of steel plates pierced with portholes, alternating with a steel trellis decorated to resemble wrought iron balconies, appears to have no artistic pedigree.

The sales rooms were renovated in 1980, and the facility looks a bit drab. Above ground level, the floors are covered with burnt-orange carpet squares, suggesting they may need to be changed often. The walls in the viewing rooms are covered with heavy red carpeting, the better to change exhibitions easily and quickly. One room we visited was hung with twentieth-century French oil paintings. In another, an auction of old coins was under way to a packed audience, and in a third, a sale of Greek and Roman earthenware was about to begin.

There is an air of efficiency here as personnel move material, answer questions, and prepare for sales. Goods offered at auction on a recent visit included designer dresses and costume jewelry, art deco and postwar minimalist furniture, toy autos and aircraft, silver table settings with coordinated serving dishes, antique furniture and paintings, and posters, books, and toys relating to the circus. All of this, seen between 11 am and noon, was to go on sale at 2 pm.

Traditionally, women employees at Hôtel Drouot wear black skirts and blouses with red scarves, and men wear black suits with red collars. In 1860, when Sardinia ceded Savoie to France, Savoyards acquired the exclusive right to transport art objects and to handle them at auction. Since then, entry into the profession has been possible only when a vacancy occurs through retirement or resignation.

Drouot had sales of about €700 million in 2005, but competition may cut into its profits. The French Assembly passed a law in 2001 that repealed the restriction of auction sales to French nationals. Both Sotheby's and Christie's have opened sales rooms in Paris. However, Drouot is taking steps to retain its leadership, with a second site on the north side of the city (64, rue Doudeauville, 18th arrondissement) and a facility for auto sales, Drouot-Véhicules.

See also Hôtel Drouot Montaigne, page 100.

Rue Montorgueil

MARKET STREET

RUE DE TURBIGO TO RUE LEOPOLD BELLAN/
RUE SAINT-SAUVEUR, 1ST AND 2ND ARR.

🚇 LES HALLES, ETIENNE MARCEL, SENTIER

TUESDAY-SATURDAY 10 AM-6 PM; SUNDAY MORNING

STEP INTO THIS MARKET STREET AND YOU IMMEDIATELY RECOGNIZE SOMETHING DIFFERENT. IT'S A PLACE OF GREAT contrasts: modern businesses housed in ancient buildings, chic shoppers stepping over dozing drunks. The white marble sidewalk pavers seem oddly out of place. Aromas of bread and coffee are adrift (stop for a croissant and a *grand café crème* at the Brasserie/Bar Compas d'Or). The scale of the buildings is low and regular, giving a feeling of an old city. Cutout metal signs at the second-floor level are reminiscent of the symbols of medieval guilds.

There are shops of every kind here: butcher shops and bakeries (*charcuteries* and *patisseries*), laundries and dry cleaners, locksmiths and shoemakers—everything you need, at fair and reasonable prices. If you're staying in the heart of Paris, this will be your market street, and perhaps your restaurant street as well: there are more than twenty to choose from.

Though not the prettiest place in Paris, rue Montorgueil is among the most legitimate. The unemployed dart rough glances at passersby, and beggars importune or nod in doorways. There is a mixture of young

mothers with babies and old women with shopping carts searching for the best produce, their spouses dutifully lugging baskets. Well-dressed urbanites grab a sandwich or rush from one appointment to another. As the day wanes, ladies of the evening appear in the alleys leading to the sex shops and peep shows in rue Saint-Denis.

Young people, as always, are looking for action, and this is a street where something is always happening. Boys on skateboards, bicycle messengers, motorcyclists who believe that any level surface is made for their convenience—all these and more conspire to keep strollers alert.

Look into l'Escargot Montorgueil at number 38. In addition to their wonderful signboard topped by a huge golden snail, they have an appealing and modestly priced lunch menu and the dark wood and polished brass of a truly old-style bistro.

We had lunch at Au Rocher de Cancale, number 78, in what might be the oldest building on the street. The peeling facade, which appears to be held up by no more than its history, is conceived in a style originated by the ancient Romans in stone. At its north end rue Montorgueil becomes rue des Petits Carreaux, a block of small shops and restaurants. A shop called simply Louis looked like a good spot for a quick sandwich, with bread baked on the premises.

Village Saint-Paul

SAINT-PAUL ANTIQUE VILLAGE

RUE SAINT-PAUL NEAR RUE CHARLEMAGNE, 4TH ARR.

🚇 SAINT-PAUL

TUESDAY-SUNDAY 9 AM-NOON, 2 PM-6 PM;

some shops may open later

ABOUT THIRTY SMALL SHOPS ARE HOUSED IN RENOVATED RESIDENTIAL BUILDINGS ON THE RIGHT BANK OF THE Seine, behind the church of Saint-Paul and Saint-Louis. Enter on rue Charlemagne, where you will be guided to the center of this little village by small purple flags announcing Village Saint-Paul. The setting is rather plain and severe, but the shops have a variety of interesting goods: Cassiopée for silver and porcelain, and Kiosk for stemware and glass pitchers.

Le Souris Vert is a sweet small shop with an offbeat collection of linens and a whole ark full of ceramic animals. The inner courtyards, paved with large granite bricks, are quiet and pleasant to saunter in. Across rue Saint-Paul is a lovely little English-language bookshop, the Red Wheelbarrow, run by two Canadian couples. You can find here all the latest books on Paris and its thousand and one delights.

Carrousel du Louvre

CARROUSEL SHOPPING CENTER

RUE DE RIVOLI AT RUE DE L'ECHELLE, 1ST ARR.

🚇 PALAIS ROYAL-MUSÉE DU LOUVRE

TUESDAY-SUNDAY 10 AM-6 PM;

some shops close from noon until 2 pm or later

AFTER YOU SPEND SOME TIME IN THE LOUVRE DES ANTI-QUAIRES, WALK ACROSS RUE DE RIVOLI TO THE CARROUSEL du Louvre for an entirely different shopping experience. This enormous space was excavated beneath the Jardin du Carrousel when the Louvre was renovated some years ago. It's one of the largest indoor shopping spaces in Paris, distinctly and even aggressively modern. Descend from rue de Rivoli into an immensity of polished marble with a grandiose feeling that depends for its effect not only on height and openness, but also on the quality of the materials. Commercial calculations must have been ignored when the Carrousel was designed.

On the main floor are a number of fine shops, French and foreign, including some good places to look for gifts: a necktie for a father or favorite uncle; a wonderful fountain pen or leather-covered writing pad for a friend; and clever toys for children. Sephora sells perfumes and beauty products of all the famous names. Glass jewelry at Salurati is unusual but expensive. The biggest shop is a Virgin Megastore that sells CDs and books interesting to students of the French language.

One of the best selections of things small and light enough to take home can be found at JNF Productions, near the Tuileries exit. Note a stunning little pocket mirror for €6; playing cards with Magritte reproductions for €7.50; notepads with art reproductions on the covers; refrigerator magnets taken from the work of famous artists; and large black and white posters for €4. Desk calendars with wonderful photo collections are available long before the coming year, and there is a very good postcard selection with unusual images.

Three well-organized and efficient restaurants are on the mezzanine. One has white tablecloths and will require a reservation, if only half an hour ahead. Two others are cafeteria-style; the lines never seem excessively long, and the food selection compares favorably with that of our favorite café in the basement of Fauchon.

Not everyone knows that the Carrousel has a separate ticket booth and entrance to the Louvre. One can often avoid the long line of people waiting to enter through the I. M. Pei glass pyramid. There are also meeting rooms, toilet facilities (not easy to find in the middle of Paris), an underground parking garage, and access to the beautifully restored and lighted foundations of the fourteenth-century wall that once surrounded the city. The display is free, and there are places to sit quietly with coffee and a sandwich while contemplating these massive and moody subterranean structures.

Passages Couverts

GALERIE COLBERT-GALERIE VIVIENNE
connecting rue des Petits-Champs, rue Vivienne,
and rue de la Banque, 2nd arr.

🚇 BOURSE

PASSAGE DU GRAND CERF
connecting rue Saint-Denis and rue Dussoubs, 2nd arr.

🚇 ETIENNE MARCEL

PASSAGE JOUFFROY-PASSAGE VERDEAU
connecting boulevard Montmartre and rue de Provence, 9th arr.

🚇 RICHELIEU-DROUOT

TUESDAY-SATURDAY 10 AM-6 PM, SUNDAY MORNING;
some shops close from noon until 2 pm or later

ON A COLD, RAINY DAY THERE IS ALWAYS SOMETHING TO SEE, BUY, EAT, OR DO IN THE COVERED PASSAGES OF PARIS. THEY originated in the period after the fall of Napoleon and during the restoration of the House of Bourbon. A new industrial class was emerging, with money to spend and a taste for shopping. At that time the city had no sewers or paved streets, and these narrow, roofed walkways provided an agreeable experience for the wealthy. By the mid-nineteenth century there were more than 150 such passages, elegantly decorated, many covered with glass roofs, and offering food and drink, billiards, public baths, and private rooms for carnal pleasures.

The *galeries*, as they are also called in French, began to decline with the arrival of the first modern department store, Au Bon Marché, which opened in 1852. Today only eighteen covered passages remain, many of them near the Palais Royal and within walking distance of the Jardin des Tuileries. One of our favorites for elegance of design and the quality of its shops is Galerie Colbert–Galerie Vivienne, connecting rue des Petits-Champs, rue Vivienne, and rue de la Banque. A charming tearoom, Priori-Thé, is a good spot for restoring the body after a morning of window-shopping. There is also a fine bookshop, to mention only two of several attractions.

Passage du Grand Cerf, not far from the Beaubourg Museum and the Conservatoire des Art et Métiers, connects the rue Saint-Denis and the rue Dussoubs. It has a great sense of style and a bright and airy ambience. Lacy ironwork supports the glass roof, and the simple black and white tile floor gives one the feeling of being in a Renaissance painting. Retail shops offer imaginative toys, hats, and jewelry. The area is a walker's delight, as surrounding streets are closed to car and truck traffic, except for deliveries.

Passage Jouffroy-Verdeau begins on the north side of boulevard Montmartre and goes straight through to rue de Provence. Spend a few minutes in Grenier à Livres, where you can turn the pages of fine old books, skim some new ones as well, and find colorful and amusing calendars. You may stop for a bite of lunch at the pleasant Restaurant Verdeau or the tiny, authentic Bistro Verdeau.

Peek into the Hôtel Chopin, no bigger than a mouse, with its fine nineteenth-century facade. Next door is the Musée Grévin, a wax museum of historical and contemporary figures to rival Madame Tussaud's in London, plus distorting mirrors and a magic show for kids of all ages. Pain d'Epice has toys and fanciful stuffed figures. The adjacent Comptoir de Famille sells bowls, baskets, hand towels, and oil and vinegar cruets.

These intriguing passages are tucked away in parts of the central city where you may search for them, or simply stumble on one or another. Not all are bright and clean, but almost every one will have a surprise or two.

BEST SHOPPING STREETS

EVERYONE DREAMS OF FREQUENTING THE GLAMOROUS SHOPS IN PARIS, AND WE ACTUALLY DID IT RESEARCHING THIS BOOK. Avenue Montaigne (8th arrondissement) is the ritziest shopping street in Paris, with the high-end Drouot auction house and all the big names in fashion—Chanel, Dior, Ungaro, and others. It's a leisurely walk from the toney Hôtel George V and the refurbished Hôtel Plaza Athénée with its three-star Alain Ducasse restaurant. Even if you're not staying in one of these hotels it's a kick to stroll through their lobbies to see who does.

The rue du Faubourg Saint-Honoré is among the longest streets in Paris, beginning at the place des Ternes in the 8th arrondissement and continuing to the place de Navarre in the 1st. This is one of the great shopping streets of the world. Addresses of interest begin at place Beauvau in front of the Elysée Palace and continue to rue Boissy d'Anglas.

Guests at the Ritz and Meurice frequent the fine shops along rue Saint-Honoré. There are many important boutiques on this street—Hermès is perhaps the leading name. A short block to the north are rue Royale, place de la Madeleine, and place Vendôme, home to wonderful shops full of expensive treasures such as jewelry, perfume, and rare foods.

On the left bank, rue de Rennes in the 6th arrondissement has strong credentials. The sidewalks bustle, the shops are welcoming and not too large, and there is a mixture of big names along with small, trendy places that change ownership frequently. Many of the high-fashion shops on the right bank have opened elegant boutiques here, and there are bookstores and art galleries as well.

Sometimes it's refreshing to go where there are fewer shops and less pressure but attractive and well-made goods. Place des Victoires and the adjacent place des Petits-Pères (2nd arrondissement) are rarely crowded. We discovered here a boutique called Question de Peau, which specializes in leather handbags and silk scarves.

Place des Vosges (4th arrondissement) has a number of fine art and antique shops under its long, cool colonnade, and some high-end boutiques such as Issey Miyake. In recent years, this part of Paris (called the Marais, as it was once a swamp) has become populated with small, interesting shops, mainly around the Musée Picasso and along rue des Francs Bourgeois.

Avenue Victor Hugo, in the 16th arrondissement between the Arc de Triomphe and place Jean Monnet, has been quietly luxurious for years, and it still seems so. It's less intense than rue de Rennes and less dramatic than avenue Montaigne, but it is an agreeable place to wander and admire the window displays, even in you don't go inside.

We haven't mentioned avenue des Champs-Elysées in the 8th arrondissement because all visitors to Paris will surely find themselves at one time or another on this fabled avenue, though to tell the truth it seems to us a bit vulgar. Still, some things just can't be found elsewhere, such as a brand of perfume called Fracas available only in Sephora, the huge cosmetics shop. But when all is said and done, your exploration of the great shopping avenues of Paris would be incomplete without a stroll down the Champs-Elysées, perhaps even a stop for coffee and a croissant.

Wine Bars

PARIS MAY NOT BE THE CAPITAL OF THE WINE WORLD (THAT'S BORDEAUX) BUT IT IS AN EXTREMELY IMPORTANT WINE CITY. Every restaurant, bistro, and brasserie has a wine list designed to complement its food. Some restaurant cellars are so highly regarded that clients come for the wine rather than the food. At wine bars throughout the city you can sample wine by the glass or try several different wines in the course of a meal.

During times when we spent many weeks in a Paris apartment, one of the places where we became regular customers was a wine shop called LA DERNIERE GOUTTE, 6, rue de Bourbon le Château, 6th arrondissement. Its American founder, Juan Sanchez, has created a niche by offering wines at modest prices from independent owner-winemakers. There is a tasting at the shop every Saturday from March through July.

HERE ARE SOME ADDITIONAL SUGGESTIONS:

RELAIS CHABLISIEN, 9, rue Bertin Poirée, 1st arr. (Métro: Pont Neuf), has enhanced its atmosphere with dark wood, checked tablecloths, and an enticing menu.

LE RUBIS, 10, rue du Marché Saint-Honoré, 1st arr. (Métro: Tuileries, Pyramides), is a busy workingman's place, with a few small tables and a simple menu. It can be identified by its row of wine barrels, covered with red-checked cloths, on the sidewalk.

AU BISTRO, just across the alley from Le Rubis, is smaller still, with a wine bar and wine to go.

WILLI'S WINE BAR, 13, rue des Petits Champs, 1st arr. (Métro: Pyramides), has a vast repertoire, good offerings of Rhône and Australian wines, and an enticing food menu.

L'ECLUSE, 15, place de la Madeleine, 8th arr. (Métro: Madeleine), specializes in Bordeaux wines. This chain of shops with the same ownership and name includes: 15, quai des Grands-Augustins, 6th arr.; 64, rue François 1er, 8th arr.; 13, rue de la Roquette, 11th arr.; 1, rue d'Armaillé, 17th arr.

JACQUES MÉLAC, 42, rue Léon Frot, 11th arr. (Métro: Charonne), has acquired a reputation for his food as well as wine, served in a pleasantly informal atmosphere.

LE BARON ROUGE, 1, rue Théophile Rossel, 12th arr. (Métro: Ledru-Rollin), behind the Beauvau covered market, is a source of wine in the barrel. To buy it you need your own bottle or plastic container. Wine and oyster feasts (in season; see page 110) that spill out onto the sidewalk start at noon on weekends.

LUCIEN LEGRAND, Filles et Fils, Galerie Vivienne, 2nd arr. (Métro: Bourse, Pyramides), has everything for the wine connoisseur: beautiful stemware, elegant carafes, and a large variety of corkscrews.

OTHER POSSIBILITIES:

LE PASSAGE, 18, Passage de la Bonne-Graine, 11th arr.

LE CAFÉ DE PASSAGE, 12, rue de Charonne, 11th arr.

LA MUSE VIN, 101, rue de Charonne, 11th arr.

LE CHAPEAU MELON, 92, rue Rébeval, 19th arr.

LA TAVERNE HENRI IV, 13, place du Pont Neuf, 1st arr.

AUTOUR D'UN VERRE, 21, rue de Trévise, 9th arr.

LA CRÉMERIE CAVES MIARD, 9, rue des Quatre-Vents, 6th arr.

LE BARATIN, 3, rue Jouye-Rouve, 20th arr.

Right Bank Markets

1st, 2nd, 3rd, and 4th arrondissements

ART, ANTIQUE, AND FLEA MARKETS

✦

LOUVRE DES ANTIQUAIRES *See page 21*
2, place Palais Royale, 1st arr. • 🚇 *Palais Royal-Musée du Louvre*
Tuesday-Sunday 10 am-6 pm;
some shops may open later and close from noon-2 pm or after

VILLAGE SAINT-HONORÉ
91, rue Saint-Honoré, 1st arr. • 🚇 *Louvre-Rivoli*
Tuesday-Sunday 10 am-6 pm;
some shops close from noon-2 pm or later

Though it is the smallest of the antique villages, with only ten shops, this collection of dealers is in some respects the most picturesque. It occupies a cul-de-sac in an old and faded part of Paris. A lovely little tearoom with a few outdoor tables makes it worth a look, if not a break for a cup of tea.

VILLAGE SAINT-PAUL *See page 30*
rue Saint-Paul near rue Charlemagne, 4th arr.
🚇 *Saint-Paul* • *Tuesday-Sunday 9 am-noon, 2-6 pm*
some shops may open later

HÔTEL DRUOUT RICHELIEU *See page 23*
9, rue Drouot, 9th arr. • 🚇 *Richelieu Drouot*
Viewing: daily 11 am-6 pm; Auctions: Monday-Friday 2-6 pm

OPEN-AIR FOOD MARKETS

✦

BAUDOYER

Place Baudoyer, 4th arr. • 🚇 *Hôtel de Ville*
Wednesday 3-8 pm, Saturday 7 am-3 pm

The market is held in front of the 4th arrondissement town hall. Alain Balmet has organic breads. In addition, there are stands selling meat, fish, and vegetables, as well as a deli offering ready-to-eat meals such as paella, chicken thighs, and ribs.

SAINT-HONORÉ

Place du Marché Saint-Honoré, 1st arr. • 🚇 *Tuileries, Pyramides*
Wednesday 3-8 pm; Saturday 7 am-3 pm

This small market was established in 2004 to serve the needs of central Paris. It is tiny compared to most open-air food markets, but there is at least one stand each for meat, fish, vegetables, and cheese.

COVERED FOOD MARKET

✦

ENFANTS ROUGES
39, rue de Bretagne, 3rd arr.
🚇 *Filles du Calvaire, Saint-Sébastien-Froissart*
Tuesday-Thursday 9 am-2 pm, 4 pm-8 pm;
Friday-Saturday 9 am-8 pm; Sunday 8:30 am-2 pm

The oldest covered market site in Paris, Enfants Rouges was established in 1628 and named for the children dressed in red who were cared for in the orphanage here. The market was closed in the 1980s and the site scheduled for other uses, but an outcry from local residents saved it. The reconstructed Enfants Rouges is clean and orderly. Its fifty stands (more outside in the street during fine weather) have galvanized hoods, and a glass roof over the whole space keeps out the rain (but not the cold). For residents in the city center, it is a vital facility, but it lacks the charm of the covered market it replaced.

MARKET STREET

✦

RUE MONTORGEUIL *See page 26*
Rue de Turbigo to rue Léopold Bellan/rue Saint-Sauveur,
1st and 2nd arr.
🚇 *les Halles, Etienne Marcel, Sentier*
Tuesday-Saturday, 10 am-6 pm; Sunday morning

OTHER MARKETS

✦

MARCHÉ AUX ANIMAUX ET AUX PLANTES
Quai de la Mégisserie from rue Lavandières
to rue du Bourdonnais, 1st arr.
🚇 *Châtelet, Pont Neuf.* • *Daily 10 am-6 pm*
Animal lovers come here to look and to dream.

MARCHÉ AUX FLEURS ET AUX OISEAUX *See page 17*
Place Louis Lépine, Île de la Cité, 1st arr.
🚇 *Cité.* • *Flowers: Monday-Saturday 9 am-6 pm*
Birds: Sunday 8 am-1 pm

LES BOUQUINISTES *See page 61*
Quai du Louvre to quai des Célestins, 2nd and 4th arr.;
quai Voltaire to quai de la Tournelle, 5th and 6th arr.
🚇 *Châtelet, Saint-Michel, Saint-Michel-Notre Dame*
Tuesday-Friday 2-6 pm; Saturday-Sunday 11 am-6 pm;
summer 9:30 am-7 pm

CARROUSEL DU LOUVRE *See page 32*
Rue de Rivoli at rue de l'Echelle, 1st arr.
🚇 *Palais Royal-Musée du Louvre*
Tuesday-Sunday 10 am-6 pm; some shops close from noon-2 pm or later

COVERED PASSAGES

✦

GALERIE COLBERT-GALERIE VIVIENNE,

connecting rue des Petits-Champs, rue Vivienne,
and rue de la Banque, 2nd arr. • 🚇 *Bourse*

PASSAGE DU GRAND CERF,

connecting rue Saint-Denis and rue Dussoubs, 2nd arr.
🚇 *Etienne Marcel*

PASSAGE JOUFFROY-PASSAGE VERDEAU,

connecting boulevard Montmartre and rue de Provence, 9th arr.
🚇 *Richelieu-Drouot*
Tuesday-Saturday 10 am-6 pm, Sunday morning;
some shops close from noon until 2 pm or later
See page 35

SQUARE DU TEMPLE

Temple Square, bounded by rue Perrée, rue de Bretagne, rue Spuller,
and rue Cafferelli, 3rd arr. • 🚇 *Temple*
Tuesday-Saturday 9 am-12:30 pm; Sunday and holidays 9 am-1 pm

In a former covered food market in front of the 3rd arrondissement town hall, this off-beat clothing market features leather jackets, sweaters, and men's suits, some new and some used.

PARIS CENTER–LEFT BANK

5th, 6th and 7th arrondissements
Le Quartier Latin, Saint-Germain-des-Prés

MARKETPLACES

Carré Rive Gauche des Antiquaires · 51
Left Bank Antique and Art Dealers

Carré des Arts Saint-Germain · 54
Saint-Germain Art and Antique Dealers

Village Suisse des Antiquités · 56
Swiss Village Antiques

Les Bouquinistes · 61
Booksellers along the Seine

FOOD MARKETS

Carré Rive Gauche des Antiquaires

LEFT BANK ANTIQUE AND ART DEALERS

IN THE AREA BOUNDED BY THE QUAI VOLTAIRE, RUE DE
L'UNIVERSITÉ, RUE DES SAINTS-PÉRES, AND RUE DU BAC, 7TH
ARR.

🚇 RUE DU BAC

TUESDAY-SUNDAY 10 AM-6 PM

some shops close from noon–2 pm or later

THESE STREETS ARE HOME TO ONE OF THE MOST EXCLUSIVE AND EXPENSIVE DECORATIVE ART MARKETS IN EUROPE. Scores of shops in the narrow streets behind the Musée d'Orsay offer every kind of antique: sculptures, paintings, rugs, tapestries, furniture, porcelain, and glass, to mention only the most familiar. Though antiques are dominant, there are a few fine art galleries and shops with contemporary goods, such as books, prints, and table linens. The antiques represent not only Europe, but also the Middle East and Far East.

A majority of the shops display over their doors a flag divided into seven colored rectangles and bearing the words "Carré Rive Gauche" to show that they are members of a merchants' association. However, a number of the shops in the area are not members, so the total concentration of dealers here is fully as impressive as the collection across the river at the Louvre des Antiquaires. Another important difference results from location: on a fine day it's agreeable to wander the narrow streets of the Carré. On cold, rainy days, the indoor Louvre has an advantage.

There is such a diversity of merchandise to look at, ponder, and crave that the neighborhood deserves a lengthy visit—or several visits. For those wishing to linger in the pleasant little streets, cafés and restaurants abound. There are also some small hotels from which one can set out early and come home to rest tired feet and ponder new discoveries.

One of our best moments came when we stumbled on the gallery that represents the cartoonist Sempé. His whimsical drawings have appeared on many *New Yorker* magazine covers, and his cartoons inside. We chose one of his drawings for our home. The dealer is Galerie Martine Gossieaux, 56, rue de l'Université, 7th arrondissement, 01 45 44 48 55, Tuesday-Saturday 2:30-7 pm (email: galerie-martine-gossieaux@wanadoo.fr).

Carré des Arts Saint-Germain

SAINT-GERMAIN ART AND ANTIQUE DEALERS

IN THE AREA BOUNDED BY QUAI MALAQUAIS, QUAI CONTI,
QUAI DES GRANDS AUGUSTINS, AND BOULEVARD SAINT-
GERMAIN, 5TH ARR.

🚇 SAINT-MICHEL, CLUNY-LA SORBONNE, ODÉON
TUESDAY-SUNDAY 10 AM-6 PM;
some shops close from noon–2 pm or later

THIS COLLECTION OF MORE THAN A HUNDRED GALLERIES AND SHOPS IS LOCATED ON THE LEFT BANK OF THE SEINE IN a group of narrow, interconnected streets. As in the Carré des Antiquaires, dealers have created a merchants' association that sponsors events to focus attention on the fine arts they sell, including contemporary two-dimensional paintings, sculpture, home decoration, and movie posters. It would be unfair to single out one vendor for our praise, but we have found work that pleased us at prices we could afford.

Within the Carré are twelve small streets, some pleasant and quiet, where window-shopping can be freely indulged, others busy with bus and car traffic. At any given time a few galleries will have shows in progress, which you are welcome to visit. Don't hesitate to go in, say *bonjour*, and look around. Often you'll be greeted in English and asked about your interests. When leaving, be sure to say "*Merci, au revoir.*" It's expected, and you'll feel welcome when you come again.

Village Suisse des Antiquités

SWISS VILLAGE ANTIQUES

AVENUE DE SUFFREN BETWEEN RUE DUPLEIX AND
AVENUE DE LA MOTTE PIQUET, 7TH ARR.

🚇 LA MOTTE PIQUET-GRENELLE
THURSDAY-MONDAY 10 AM-7 PM

PARIS IS FULL OF LITTLE VILLAGES, FROM CLUSTERS OF MEWS-LIKE HOUSES TO VAST APARTMENT COMPLEXES. THE term is also used to describe groups of antique shops where a number of vendors gain identity (and sales) from a common location. There are two such *villages* along the rue Saint-Honoré, in the northern 16th arrondissement, and in the 4th arrondissement near the Seine. Village Suisse is just west of the École Militaire, and a brisk walk from the Eiffel Tower. It's open on weekdays, when Clignancourt is closed.

Village Suisse has much to offer both the casual visitor and the serious collector. It comprises more than one hundred fifty shops on the ground level (and a few below) of two large, modern apartment buildings. The area is clean, nicely planted with trees and flowers, and supplied with outdoor benches. It has a large variety of specialty boutiques offering such rarities as nautical instruments and models, glass miniatures, and pipes and smoking materials. The quality of the merchandise appears to be high, and the vendors are friendly and knowledgeable.

We found a huge marble mortar in one shop here, and a tiny blue stone cow in another, items that whetted our appetite for something

CONSULAT

unique to take home—exactly what Village Suisse can provide. In addition, 78, Le Kepi Rouge, has an impressive collection of weapons, toy soldiers, and military paintings. Jeanne et Jeremy sell handmade dolls. Fireplace tools at number 16–18 are far from ordinary. Catherine Hirsch at number 28 specializes in clocks; and one should at least admire the Empire furniture at En 95.

Period furniture, especially from the late nineteenth and early twentieth centuries, is a strong element in this *village*. It may not be what you came for, but it could turn out to be what you take home.

Les Bouquinistes

BOOKSELLERS ALONG THE SEINE

QUAI DU LOUVRE TO QUAI DES CÉLESTINS,

2ND AND 4TH ARR.; QUAI VOLTAIRE

TO QUAI DE LA TOURNELLE, 5TH AND 6TH ARR.

🚇 CHÂTELET, SAINT-MICHEL, SAINT-MICHEL-NOTRE DAME

TUESDAY-FRIDAY 2 PM-6 PM; SATURDAY-SUNDAY 11 AM-6 PM;

SUMMER 9:30 AM-7 PM

BOOKSELLERS ALONG THE SEINE CAME INTO EXISTENCE IN THE MID-SIXTEENTH CENTURY. AT THAT TIME, TO PREVENT them from selling forbidden Protestant pamphlets they were required to have a royal patent. They spread out their goods on the Pont Neuf, the first bridge built over the river Seine (completed in 1606). After the 1789 Revolution, entire libraries seized from noble families or the clergy ended up for sale on the bridges of Paris.

The ancestors of today's green boxes were wooden trays attached to the bridge parapets with leather straps. In 1891 the *bouquinistes* received permission from the government to hang permanent boxes along the sidewalks bordering the Seine. Each dealer is subject to restrictions regarding the number of boxes (four), the total space occupied (eight meters), and the color of the boxes (dark green),

A casual passerby might take this for a market of the mundane, but a closer inspection reveals everything from the ponderous to the arcane, from the titillating to the outrageous. Serious materials shade off into tourist-oriented stuff, which is said to provide an increasingly important source of income for these vendors. There are currently 250 of them, and one hears that the waiting time to enter the trade is eight years.

The *bouquinistes* are an important resource for collectors of rare botanical prints and early editions. In fact, secondhand books are a mainstay of the trade (the number available is estimated at three hundred thousand), though they are less obvious than magazines, posters, prints, cards, and engravings. All are stocked (and locked) in the long, lugubrious-looking dark green boxes that straddle the walls overlooking the Seine.

Business hours of the *bouquinistes* are anything but predictable, though the vendors are supposed to be open at least four days a week. A typical day in the off-season is likely to find half of them at work, while a sunny summer day may bring out nearly all.

Whatever the case, they're an established part of the market scene in Paris, and worth an hour's investigation, especially if one has a purpose. We're interested in food and cooking, and we found a lot to look at on the quai de Conti on the left bank, opposite the rue de Guénégaud. Out-of-print cookbooks, old menus, and blank menus for dinner parties were for sale here.

Don't overlook the *bouquinistes* on the right bank (north side) of the river. One of them offers a variety of small plaques (about 4 by 6 inches) called *metals*, with historic advertising images in full color, of brands such as Coca-Cola, Camel cigarettes, Lu biscuits, and Absinthe.

Rue Mouffetard

MARKET STREET

FROM RUE THOUIN TO RUE EDOUARD QUÉNU AND
RUE CENSIER, 5TH ARR.

🚇 MONGE, CENSIER DAUBENTON

TUESDAY-SATURDAY 10 AM-6 PM; SUNDAY MORNING

SOME PEOPLE SAY THEY'RE NOT REALLY IN PARIS UNTIL THEY'RE BACK IN RUE MOUFFETARD. THE COBBLESTONE surface, the gentle turns as the street weaves down the hill behind the Panthéon, and the narrowness of the street combine to give Mouffetard its somewhat medieval aspect. No structure is much over six or seven stories high. There's been an effort to clean, paint, and repair, but many buildings still have the peeling facades that give the place its venerable appearance. It's not hard to see why it's thought by some to be the quintessential Paris market street, even though it's sometimes overwhelmed by tourists.

The pedestrian part of the street starts at the vehicle barrier at rue Calvin. Near the uphill end, at place de la Contrescarpe, a central fountain is surrounded in the spring by a ring of bright impaties. On the south side, Café Delmas is crowded when sunshine is the priority. When it gets hot, Café Contrescarpe across the square is nicely shaded and busy in its turn.

Along the winding descent are a number of small produce stands, along with fishmongers, bakeries, and *patisseries*, each with a faith-

ful clientele and a unique presentation. In autumn, a butcher specializing in game has an incredible display of birds. La Toscane, the Italian grocer, makes wonderful pastas and sells the most desirable Italian cheeses all year long.

Small restaurants offer half a dozen national foods, from Greek gyros to Japanese sushi. If none of these appeals, there are crêperies and sandwich shops. Au Piano Muet at number 48 presents an appealing and reasonably priced lunch menu. L'Huitre et Demie at number 78 has a tiny dining room (seven tables) and a tempting menu. Au Petit Bistro across the street offers a classic environment and a choice of dependable dishes.

The confined character of the street gives a special intensity to commerce here, as shoppers and merchants meet nose to nose. The last produce stand at the bottom of the hill is Pomi V, opposite the church in the square Saint-Médard. Self-service is the model, which makes shopping fast and efficient. Perfect pyramids of strawberries, apples, kiwis, and oranges are demolished by determined shoppers as noon approaches.

When you emerge at this end of the street, few things could be more appealing than half an hour's respite and a glass of wine or a pastis at Cave la Bourgogne, with its pleasant outlook and traditional atmosphere, on the corner of rue Edouard Quénu.

Marché Saxe-Breteuil

OPEN-AIR MARKET

AVENUE DE SAXE FROM PLACE DE BRETEUIL

TO AVENUE DE SÉGUR, 7TH ARR.

🚊 SÉGUR, DUROC

THURSDAY 7 AM-2:30 PM; SATURDAY 7 AM-3 PM

WHEN WE CONJURE UP IMAGES OF THE MOST APPEALING OUTDOOR FOOD MARKETS IN PARIS, ONE OF THE FIRST that comes to mind is Saxe-Breteuil. This is a neighborhood of well-to-do residents, and the vendors understand that their clients are discriminating and have money to spend, which helps explain the quality of meat, fish, and produce, as well as the wide range of other products.

The market is shaded in summer by two rows of sycamore trees. Tall light poles with modern fixtures provide a bit of architectural glamour. The Eiffel Tower is always in view, which adds to the pleasure. On clear summer mornings, sunshine floods down avenue de Saxe from place de Breteuil, suffusing the whole market with a golden glow.

With two parallel rows of stalls, it's easy to get around Saxe-Breteuil. In addition to the usual complement of food stalls, there's a mind-numbing assortment of household goods: fine lace tablecloths, scented soaps, Oriental carpets, quilts, and hardware, all well displayed and of good quality. Jackeye and Marcel Deshaies bring fresh oysters from Marennes and Oléron on the Atlantic coast. Marcel will explain the fine points of difference among *fines de claires*, *speciales*, and *belons*.

Personal clothing is abundant: blouses, sweaters, shirts, and shoes, as well as leather jackets and raincoats. Purses, wallets, and other leather goods known as *maroquinerie* (because they come from Morocco) are displayed at one stand. At another are wood boxes made from the root of the *thuya* or Tetraclinis tree. Did anyone ever hear of it? It's also worth looking at Paul Ostrowski's array of stemware and glass vases, whose shapes are both interesting and artful. A bit difficult to carry or ship, but his prices are irresistible.

To round out the offerings, there are Teflon cooking pots, toy cars, dolls' clothing, and socks for sensitive feet. It's worth noting that the clientele are well dressed and considerate of others. Sources report that former Prime Minister Balladur sometimes shops here, adding one more element of human interest to this rich and wonderful market.

Marché Monge

OPEN-AIR MARKET

PLACE MONGE, 5TH ARR.

🚇 MONGE

WEDNESDAY, FRIDAY 7 AM-2:30 PM, SUNDAY 7 AM-3 PM

MARCHÉ MONGE IS CONVENIENTLY LOCATED IN THE HEART OF THE LEFT BANK. WE SHOPPED HERE MANY TIMES WHEN we rented an apartment on the rue de Buci, and we found the best of what we needed for our daily meals: bread and cheese, meat and fish, herbs and spices, and the seasonal fruits and vegetables that make the open-air food markets one of Paris's most attractive features. The Métro is handy (two entrances on the east side of the square), and the spacing of stalls makes it easy to get around. Under an immense umbrella of plane trees, the summer market is cool and welcoming.

There is a soft litter underfoot of seeds from the trees when we emerge from the Métro. As always, a long line is waiting at the vegetable stand of P. Casson. His carrots have vigorous green tops, and dirt still clings to their skins. Fat celery roots look like models of alien planets, and pumpkins are sliced open to expose entrails the color of an August moon. Stalks of rhubarb are as large as walking sticks, and a fork sticks up from a cooked beet the size of a softball; buyers select and spear their choice.

In retail shops it's bad form to touch the produce; rather, you wait to be served, then point out or describe to the salesperson what you want (often agony for a foreigner). But in the open-air markets, you take a plastic basket or tin pan, fill it with whatever you choose, and hand it to the vendor to be weighed and priced. To make it totally simple, get in line, watch what other people do, and copy them.

M. Chau sells tomatoes, endives, and a dazzling variety of lettuces, made more tantalizing by a light sprinkling of water. Everything is perfectly ripe. Perhaps we'll buy a frisée lettuce here: one of our favorite dishes is sautéed onions and chicken livers with frisée, and a chilled rosé wine to wash it down.

Catherine and Giles LeGall, *ostreiculteurs* from Brittany, bring sea-farmed shellfish a few hours from their element. To allay our disappointment after we've rejected some cracked and broken mussels, Giles breaks open a fresh bag. We'll cook them in a broth of white wine with chopped onion, tomato, and parsley; this classic Belgian dish, *moules marinières*, is usually served with French fries.

There's a new addition when we visit in the spring: two African men are selling earrings, beads, and articles made from horn, such as salad servers and pasta spoons. Place mats made from a soft grasslike material are €12 for a set. We've seen them in upscale shops at twice that price. Not to be overlooked at Veramex are bird whistles carved from branches.

The fresh catch at *poissonnerie* Chez Loulou smells so brisk and briny that we choose a few *gambas*, enormous sweet shrimp, as a first course for our evening meal. With a loaf of country-baked bread from Lupo and a few more vegetables from Tan Sir Ti, the market basket is overflowing. Luckily, it's only a short walk to our apartment.

Marché Raspail

OPEN-AIR MARKET

BOULEVARD RASPAIL FROM RUE DU CHERCHE-MIDI
TO RUE DE RENNES, 6TH ARR.

🚊 RENNES

TUESDAY, FRIDAY 7 AM-2:30 PM; SUNDAY (ORGANIC) 7 AM-3 PM

BOULEVARD RASPAIL CUTS THROUGH THE 6TH ARRONDISSE-MENT FROM THE BOULEVARD SAINT-GERMAIN TO PLACE Denfert Rochereau, sloping gently upward as it goes south and encountering six Métro stations of four different lines. Three times a week one of the most attractive food markets in Paris opens here. It's spitting rain the first time we go, so the stalls are under canvas or metal awnings. But despite the weather and the small number of shoppers, the horn of plenty is overflowing and the vendors are their usual charming selves.

At the biggest and most pristine of the *charcuterie* stands we strike up a conversation with Madame Gache, a small, energetic woman with bright black eyes and rough, red hands. She offers a full array of pork products, everything prepared at home. We ask how the open-air markets are doing in the face of competition from the supermarkets. "Look around," she says with a sweep of her hand. "All these older people grew up with the open markets. But where are the young ones? If we don't see them soon, we'll all be out of business."

We're staying in a hotel on this visit and have no need to buy food, so we can be more leisurely. Today, pig snouts get our attention. They're stacked in a wooden box, looking more like goblin masks than something to take home for dinner. These ghost-like objects attest to the French genius at finding a culinary use for every part of every beast.

Further reflection about snouts brings to mind a dish called *salade de museau* that we've been seeing and puzzling over in the butcher shops and delicatessens. It looks like chicken salad, but doesn't quite taste like it. Now we know the answer. Next to the snouts is a box of trotters, then tails, and beside the tails, improbably if predictably, ears. We're told they taste best when fried quickly in a little olive oil.

At a nearby stand we find fresh duck eggs, each one three to four times the size of a hen's egg and so heavy we remember the goose that laid the golden egg—that must be how the story got started. In the adjacent stall, half a dozen varieties of mushrooms are laid out, among them one new to us called sheep's foot that looks like the splayed hoof of an herbivore. And then all the glorious greens: crinkly spinach, crisp, peppery *cresson*, and our favorite *frisée*.

Once we thought the freshest fish were found in only port cities or nearby, where the trip from the sea to the dinner table might be little more than a few hours. But here is surpassing variety and abundance, fresh from both Atlantic and Mediterranean waters. Some big fellows still twitch their last on a bed of ice.

The Sunday market is *biologique* (organic), and it draws a somewhat different clientele. As always, we find good things to eat and drink, as well as some new discoveries to add to our suitcase. A table full of toys (for organic tots, of course) catches our eye; then a small stand selling (at *prix choc*, as the French describe a bargain) sticks of vanilla and the bark of wild cinnamon.

A selection of soap interests us, since we've learned that *savon de Marseille*, from the south of France, will take stains out of anything. We choose a few bars with the color and scent of olive oil. Honeycomb candles are available at home, but the price of these is not to be believed, so into the shopping bag they go, to further strain the seams of our bulging sack.

At the end of the market, a young man is frying potato cakes with onion and cheese. This looks like good picnic fare and it smells wonderful; we can't resist asking for a couple. A dozen different fruit tarts appeal to our sweet tooth, so we carry off one lemon and one rhubarb to complete our lunch al fresco in the Jardin du Luxembourg.

La Grande Épicerie, Bon Marché Rive Gauche

BON MARCHÉ FOOD HALL

RUE DE SÉVRES AT RUE DU BAC, 7TH ARR.

🚇 SÉVRES BABYLONE

MONDAY-SATURDAY 8:30 AM-9 PM

MAIN STORE: MONDAY, TUESDAY, THURSDAY, FRIDAY 9:30 AM-7 PM;

THURSDAY 10 AM-9 PM; SATURDAY 9:30 AM-8 PM

THE BON MARCHÉ DEPARTMENT STORE USED TO LOOK SOME-WHAT SHOPWORN COMPARED WITH ITS COMPETITORS ON the Right Bank: la Samaritaine (now closed), le Printemps, and especially les Galeries Lafayette's gourmet food hall. But it's the only department store of comparable scale on the left bank, and a few years ago it went through a dazzling renovation. Now all has changed for the better: a bright, clean attractive space to shop for domestic or foreign food products of superior quality.

The main building is a conventional department store, interesting in its own right if you're staying on the left bank (it's only a few steps from the Hotel Lutétia). However, the ground floor of the smaller building across the rue du Bac is the place for serious food shopping. It has bright new flooring, custom lighting, and spruced-up displays. A number of things about this place are particularly appealing: the signage is easy to see and read (though some French is required). There is an observable

logic to the organization. The ceilings are high and the aisles are wide; you can see where you are and where you want to go. Renamed La Grand Épicerie de Paris, this may be the best gourmet food market in the city, with an immense selection of exceptional and high-quality products.

Any preserved food you can think of in a box or a can is somewhere on these shelves; for example, mushrooms—canned, in liquid, dried, vacuum packed, domestic, and foreign. Fresh foods are even more impressive. The fish is artfully arranged on ice with swirls of seaweed, and it smells like a fresh Breton breeze. The meat is trimmed to perfection, each cut ready for pan or broiler, and the fruit and vegetables are polished and stacked like ammunition for a siege. On our last visit, a display of Japanese food looked as if it had come straight from the Ginza in Tokyo.

We often fill a special order at Bon Marché for friends at home: bottles of peppercorns (black, white, or five-grain) with a grinder built into the top. Sea salt from Brittany, wonderful stuff known as *la fleur de sel*, is available in the same format. But these are only two tiny samples from a vast offering.

The second floor used to house antique dealers and a couple of uninteresting restaurants. No longer: it's been refurbished with specialty clothing retailers around the perimeter, and in the center, a smart-looking fast-food restaurant called Délicabar: Snack Chic. Colorful banquettes invite a stop for a bite. A garden in the center is open to the sky, with big white hanging parasols.

The simple fact is, we go back to La Grand Épicerie again and again and are never disappointed with the experience, even if it's just to look and to buy nothing at all.

Rue Cler

MARKET STREET

RUE DE GRENELLE TO AVENUE DE LA MOTTE PICQUET, 7TH ARR.

🚇 ÉCOLE MILITAIRE

TUESDAY-SATURDAY 10 AM-6 PM; SUNDAY MORNING

RUE CLER IS A WIDE AND WELCOMING PEDESTRIAN STREET IN ONE OF THE UPSCALE PARTS OF PARIS, A MECCA FOR visitors given the proximity of the Tour Eiffel, École Militaire, and Hôtel des Invalides. But the main character of the surrounding neighborhood is residential: quiet, tree-lined streets with homes and apartments, a scattering of small shops, and an overriding sense of privileged living.

Rue Cler is like many such streets where every kind of fresh and prepared food is sold, but it is perhaps the cleanest, brightest, and best organized of all. Marble pavers laid in broad rainbow arcs are spotless. In the shops, food and produce are beautifully arranged, with out-of-season specialties like raspberries that the clientele can afford.

The quality here is uniformly excellent, and the *bûcheries* and *charcuteries* have an impressive variety of prepared meats, small roasts with diverse stuffings, and, in the fall, game birds dressed and ready for the oven. One butcher displays at least fourteen different cuts of pork, plus ears and trotters, in his glass case.

A few doors away, La Maison du Jambon is richly provisioned with hanging hams, fine wines, after-dinner drinks, and canned and prepared foods. This is as close to an American-style delicatessen as you're likely to

find in Paris. Nearby, a *fromagerie* with a straw ceiling and big wooden beams draws us in to admire a looming avalanche of cheeses.

Olivier et Compagnie at number 44 sells olive oils from around the Mediterranean. A la Mère de Famille at number 47 specializes in chocolates, but note in the window tiny enameled teapots with charming designs for €60. It will seem like a lot of money until you look closely at the quality of the decoration.

The Café du Marché, at the corner of rue du Champs de Mars, is flooded with sunshine at noon. Diners are served tasty salads and hot dishes at tables that are small and close together. We couldn't avoid overhearing conversations: stories from the office, intimate liaisons, and the inevitable discussions of European football. For a simpler meal, there's the Bar/Brasserie PTT, or if New Yorkers want to feel more at home, the TribecA is good for a sandwich and a cup of coffee.

Lionel Poilâne

8, RUE DU CHERCHE-MIDI, 6TH ARR.

MONDAY-SATURDAY 7:15 AM-8:15 PM

ONE OF THE BEST THINGS TO EAT IN PARIS—OR IN FRANCE, FOR THAT MATTER—IS BREAD. NOT JUST ORDINARY BAKERY bread, but bread made with slow-rising, natural yeast and baked in a wood-fired oven. This is the way Poilâne makes it for Parisians, for restaurants across France, and for shops around the world. Sadly, the founder died in 2002 in a helicopter accident, but his shops continue to deliver the same high level of product and service.

A stop at this delightful little shop can, if you ask, include a visit to the oven in the basement, a wood-fired giant that is partly responsible for the special quality of the product. To see it in operation, we went down a winding stone staircase, its treads hollowed by a hundred years of use. The room below, a vaulted cellar of smooth, brown limestone, was insufferably hot. One man was working alone in shorts and heavy shoes, stoking the fire, pulling baked goods in and out of the oven with the rhythm of long experience, keeping up a conversation with us all the time. He works an eight-hour shift with other bakers, so the oven is going around the clock.

This morning he was baking Poilâne's signature round loaves of sourdough bread, and *sablés*, small round tea-cookies. Like all traditional bakers, he uses a thin, flat paddle at the end of a ten-foot long handle to put loaves of bread or sheets of cookies into the oven and move them to get the best exposure to the heat.

The coolness of the next room was a relief after the heat of the ovens. Machines from another century mix and shape dough and core apples for tarts. The baker here was preparing cookies for the oven, stamping out small rounds from a sheet of dough that had been formed by a large, flat machine something like a clothes wringer. Quickly and methodically he moved them in stacks to a tray where he spread them out, ready for the oven. We calculated his rate of production at about four hundred an hour for four hours before he risked going mad.

Back in the baking room we were offered oven-fresh *sablés* to taste. They're not too sweet, but crisp and buttery with a hint of cinnamon. Big baskets of rising bread dough were stacked on racks along the walls, waiting their turn in the oven. The baker pinched off a bit so we could savor the yeasty, sour flavor for which Poilâne is justly famous. A portion of this raw dough, rather than fast-rising industrial yeast, is added to each fresh batch of flour, water, and salt to start the slow-rising process.

A friend once brought us a present from Paris. Fearing that another useless object might be about to enter our lives, we hesitantly opened the package. Imagine our delight on finding a box of Poilâne's *Punitions* (punishments), small, sweet tea cookies that have a loyal following all over the world.

Before we left, the first loaves were ready to come out of the oven. The baker lifted them one by one on his paddle and stacked them in a rack. Their aroma flooded the room, triggering a basic instinct, and we raced upstairs to get in line for our loaf.

EATING OUT IN PARIS

Everyone who goes to Paris must find meals, and one hopes they will be good ones. The problem is not that there aren't enough places to eat—in fact, there are more than four thousand of them. But the variety and subtle distinctions among them are enough to drive a visitor mad. Here's a brief guide to some basic differences.

The word *restaurant* in French does not have the same generic meaning as in English. Rather, it describes an establishment that meets certain qualifications and expectations in the minds of clients, and in the minds of government officials who award licenses. It is often a large establishment aware of its importance, and it is possibly though not necessarily expensive.

The Michelin guide, that fat red book reborn every April with restaurant and hotel rankings based on one, two, or three stars, is a good indicator of what constitutes a restaurant, though the book includes more modest establishments as well. A restaurant will have a white cloth on the table, an elaborate menu (*la carte*), and a highly professional serving staff. In most respects, it is the peak institution among French eating establishments.

The brasserie was born as a beer-hall in Alsace, the region where France and Germany share a border. It is less self-conscious about its cooking than a restaurant. Brasserie food is basic food, everything the French love, from traditional *oeuf mayonnaise* to *steak au poivre*, *pommes frites*, and *crème caramel*. The most reliable meals in Paris are available at its brasseries, continuously during open hours, late at night, on weekends, and Mondays, when most restaurants traditionally are closed.

We adore the food and ambience of the brasserie and have a special feeling for big, bustling Bofinger, rue de la Bastille in the 4th arrondissement, near where we once lived in Paris. A junior edition of Bofinger can be found across the street. The brasserie at the Hotel Lutétia, boulevard Raspail in the 6th arrondissement, may be as close to a deluxe establishment as one can find; their smoked salmon and raw oysters are celestial. Brasserie Lipp, on boulevard Saint-Germain in the 6th arrondissement since 1880, has been and still is the place to get a glimpse of France's political, artistic, and intellectual glitterati.

A bistro is usually a small, family-style restaurant, often with a lively sense of its place in the firmament. Most offer traditional fare, though there is a movement toward experimental cooking in some, such as l'Epi Dupin, rue Dupin, and les Bookinistes, quai des Grands Augustins, both in the 6th arrondissement. A classic and favorite of ours is le Bistro d'Henri, rue Princesse, in the 6th arrondissement.

The straightforward but essential café is a basic feature of alimentary and social life outside the home. There is one in nearly every block in Paris, often with tables on the sidewalk in the sun. Coffee, beer, and wine are the mainstays of the café, but simple food is also available, served quickly from a limited but hearty menu. Big, bustling places like the Deux Magots and the Flore on boulevard Saint-Germain are true cafés, but they are the racehorses of the breed, not the workhorses.

Not to be overlooked is the humble bar. Sometimes it will be the only thing in sight for a coffee and a croissant on a cold day, or to make a bathroom stop (don't expect to use the *toilettes* unless you buy a coffee). It may look dark and dingy, but a bar is a reservoir of warmth and good will for the visitor who may need it in a pinch.

Everywhere, *le menu* means the meal of the day, while *la carte* is the list of food and drink. Establishments of all kinds generally stop serving lunch by three o'clock, some earlier. And don't expect to arrive for dinner before seven-thirty or eight o'clock. If you do, you may see the kitchen and wait staff clustered around a back table enjoying a jovial meal together before work begins.

At the back of this book we've provided a list of reasonably priced restaurants, bistros, brasseries, and wine bars organized by arrondissement. We've frequented many of them, but don't take our word for it; experience will guide you to your own wonderful discoveries.

Left Bank Markets
5th, 6th, and 7th arrondissements

ART, ANTIQUE, AND FLEA MARKETS

✦

CARRÉ DES ARTS SAINT-GERMAIN *See page 54*

In the area bounded by quai Malaquais, quai Conti, quai des Grands Augustins, and boulevard Saint-Germain, 6th arr.

🚇 *Saint-Michel, Cluny-la Sorbonne, Odéon*

Tuesday-Sunday 10 am-6 pm; some shops close from noon-2 pm or later

CARRÉ RIVE GAUCHE DES ANTIQUAIRES *See page 51*

In the area bounded by the quai Voltaire, rue de l'Université, rue des Saints-Péres, and rue du Bac, 7th arr. • 🚇 *rue du Bac*

Tuesday-Sunday 10 am-6 pm; some shops close from noon-2 pm or later

VILLAGE SUISSE DES ANTIQUITÉS *See page 56*

Avenue de Suffren from rue Dupleix to avenue de la Motte Piquet, 7th arr.

🚇 *La Motte Piquet-Grenelle • Thursday-Monday 10 am-7 pm; some shops close from noon-2 pm or later*

COVERED FOOD MARKET

✦

SAINT-GERMAIN-DES-PRÉS

3, rue Mabillon, 6th arr. • 🚇 *Odéon, Mabillon*
Tuesday-Saturday 8 am-1 pm, 4-7:30 pm; Sunday 8 am-1 pm

A historic covered food market dating from 1813, the last vestige of the celebrated Saint-Germain Fair of the Middle Ages was torn down to make room for upscale clothing shops. Part of the ground floor was reconstituted as a food market and opened in 1992. The produce is fresh and beautifully displayed in a calm and pleasant atmosphere compared with the tumult of the typical Parisian market. Prices are high, but on a rainy day in the heart of the Left Bank, that may be less important than keeping dry.

✦

MAUBERT

Place Maubert, 5th arr. • 🚇 *Maubert-Mutualité*
Tuesday, Thursday 7 am-2:30 pm, Saturday 7 am-2:30 pm

A noose of trucks contains a small market around the Maubert Métro entrance. The stalls are close together, leaving scant room for shoppers to pass. Though smaller than the nearby market in place Monge, this one is energetic and eclectic. Established shops in the little square fit the pace and tone of the market.

MONGE *See page 72*

Place Monge, 5th arr.
🚇 *Monge* • *Wednesday, Friday 7 am-2:30 pm, Sunday 7 am-3 pm*

PORT ROYAL

Boulevard de Port Royal, in front of the Hôpital du Val de Grace, 5th arr.
🚇 *Port Royal* • *Tuesday, Thursday 7 am-2:30 pm, Saturday 7 am-3 pm*

Port Royal occupies a stretch of sidewalk on the south side of the Val de Grace hospital, an extraordinarily beautiful building in a large and gracious park. This small neighborhood market has the customary array of meat, fish, fowl, and produce stands, and some inexpensive clothing. Here, as in place Monge, Catherine and Gilles LeGall sell sea-farmed oysters and mussels from Brittany.

RASPAIL   *See page 75*

Boulevard Raspail from rue du Cherche-Midi to rue de Rennes, 6th arr.

🚋 *Rennes*

Tuesday, Friday 7 am-2:30 pm, Sunday (organic) 9 am-2 pm

SAXE-BRETEUIL   *See page 68*

Avenue de Saxe, from place de Breteuil to avenue de Ségur, 7th arr.

🚋 *Ségur, Duroc • Thursday 7 am-2:30 pm; Saturday 7 am-3 pm*

MARKET STREETS

✦

RUE MOUFFETARD   *See page 64*

Rue Calvin to rue Edward Quenu/rue Censier, 5th arr.

🚋 *Monge, Censier Daubenton*

Tuesday-Saturday, 10 am-6 pm; Sunday morning

RUE CLER *See page 84*

Rue de Grenelle to avenue de la Motte Picquet, 7th arr.

🚋 *École Militaire • Tuesday-Saturday 10 am-6 pm; Sunday morning*

OTHER MARKETS

✦

LA GRAND ÉPICERIE DE PARIS, BON MARCHÉ RIVE GAUCHE
See page 80
Rue de Sèvres at rue du Bac, 7th arr. • 🚇 *Sèvres Babylone*
Monday-Saturday 9 am-6 pm
Main Store: Monday, Tuesday, Wednesday, Friday 9:30 am-7 pm;
Thursday 10 am-9 pm; Saturday 9:30 am-8 pm

LES BOUQUINISTES *See page 61*
Quai du Louvre to quai des Célestins, 2nd and 4th arr.; quai Voltaire
to quai de la Tournelle, 5th and 6th arr.
🚇 *Châtelet, Saint-Michel, Saint-Michel-Notre Dame*
Tuesday-Friday 2 pm-6 pm; Saturday-Sunday 11 am-6 pm;
summer 9:30 am-7 pm

PARIS WEST

8th and 16th arrondissements

Les Invalides, Passy, Le Trocadero, l'Étoile

MARKETPLACES

Hôtel Drouot Montaigne · 100

Drouot Auction House-Montaigne

Marché aux Timbres et aux Cartes Téléphoniques · 102

Postage Stamp and Telephone Card Market

FOOD MARKETS

Marché Président Wilson · 105

Open-Air Market

✦

When in Paris, Do as the Parisians · 108

About Oysters · 110

Paris West Markets · 112

Hôtel Drouot Montaigne

15, AVENUE MONTAIGNE, 8TH ARR.

🚇 ALMA-MARCEAU

VIEWING: MONDAY-FRIDAY 11 AM-6 PM

AUCTIONS: MONDAY-FRIDAY 2-6 PM

THE LOCATION AND ARCHITECTURE HERE ARE AS DIFFERENT FROM DROUOT RICHELIEU (PAGE 23) AS FINE CHINA IS FROM five-and-dime dishware. This branch of the auction house sells high-end French furnishings and decorative arts. The building resembles a small

townhouse or a classy boutique hotel, in keeping with the neighbors in one of the most chic and expensive Parisian shopping streets. From the entrance hall of polished blond marble, a wide staircase with art nouveau banisters curves downward to a wood paneled reception area. Stylish young women in smart red suits assist legitimate visitors. We dropped in for a tour, but having no business other than being nosy travel writers, the front desk was as far as we got.

Marché aux Timbres
et aux Cartes Téléphoniques

POSTAGE STAMP AND TELEPHONE CARD MARKET

AVENUE DE MARIGNY FROM AVENUE GABRIEL TO ALLÉE
MARCEL PROUST, 8TH ARR.

🚇 CHAMPS ELYSÉES-CLEMENCEAU

THURSDAY, SATURDAY, SUNDAY, HOLIDAYS 10 AM-DUSK

IN A CITY OF LONG-ESTABLISHED MARKETS, THE POSTAGE STAMP MARKET IS ONE OF THE OLDEST. EVEN IF YOU'RE not a collector of postage stamps, an hour invested here will give you a lesson in geography and history, and demonstrate art of high quality. We were struck, for example, by the exquisite rendering of tropical birds and flowers on the stamps of Mauritius and Madagascar.

Dealers organize their material by the country of origin and subject, and the logic of organization is itself an art. In addition to stamps sold singly or in sheets, franked or un-franked, you can find postcards with their original stamps and envelopes with letters still inside them. There is a certain voyeuristic pleasure in reading reports and musings of people long ago and far away. Each time we go back we are impressed by the diligence of these vendors, who sort and classify their stamps with magnifying glasses while they wait for visits by serious collectors.

At the avenue Gabriel, stamps give way to a new type of market: used telephone cards. Since they were introduced little more than a

decade ago, phone cards carrying a small electronic *puce*, or flea, have swept across Europe. This market is still a rather informal institution compared with the stamp market, but it is growing at a brisk pace.

Dealers work on park benches, on the hoods of cars, or on their laps as they display albums and boxes of cards for sale or trade. With an enormous variety of images and graphic designs, from sports figures to musicians and artists, from history to space travel and fantasy, phone cards have quickly gained a place in the affections of collectors. They are avidly compared, traded, bought, and sold in a market that has quickly become a fixture.

Marché Président Wilson

OPEN-AIR-MARKET

AVENUE DU PRÉSIDENT WILSON FROM PLACE D'IÉNA TO RUE
DEBROUSSE, 16TH ARR.

🚇 IÉNA

WEDNESDAY, 7 AM-2:30 PM, SATURDAY, 7 AM-3 PM

TWO ROWS OF STANDS FACE EACH OTHER UNDER YOUNG ACACIA TREES THAT REPLACED AGING PLANE TREES AND are beginning to provide comfortable shade. A red and white *Rotisserie* sign near the middle of the market lends a certain sense of gaiety to this gourmet dream. It also identifies a source of roasted chicken, which the vendor puts into a foil-lined bag to send home warm. There is another source of roasted chicken, ribs, and small white potatoes at the west end of the market, but it's impossible to choose one over the other.

Well-dressed older women scout the produce, along with mothers pushing prams or leading children by the hand. A typical outfit here in autumn is a Hermès scarf over a chic sweater and skirt, worn with high heels; in spring, it's tight little jackets, blue jeans, and flat shoes. Men are casual in cashmere jackets and foulards or, if it's warm, open-neck shirts and trousers. Some shoppers carry straw market baskets, but more often we see small, two-wheeled carts, especially on rainy days.

Products not often found in other markets are available here, such as silk blouses, new books, posters, and wine at €10 a bottle compared to €4 or €5 elsewhere. In summer there are fine straw hats and cotton socks,

and often a selection of table linens by reputable makers. Duval has a full line of dried fruits and nuts to tuck away as a snack. Lafitte sells canned products from the southwest, including a superb *rillette* of duck, which you can pop into your suitcase to take home.

Choucroute arrives in September, and its tantalizing aroma pervades the market until June. Bob Hamon's Breton name gives added authenticity to his steaming pot of homemade pickled cabbage adorned with chunks of ham and sausage. Considering the mounds that are decimated in the course of a morning, we understand that many others love *choucroute* as we do.

Farther down are several flower stands, as well as honey and farm-baked bread. We like to buy goat cheese from Saint-Vrain. These vendors offer a polite *bonjour* and invite us to taste, demonstrating the courtesy that characterizes most markets. There may be as many as five fishmongers, a similar number of butchers, and as much fresh, beautifully displayed produce of excellent quality as we have seen anywhere.

Despite the stylish character and somewhat higher prices at the Marché Président Wilson, vendors here as elsewhere speed sales in the last fifteen minutes by calling out to passersby: "*Je finis la table à cinq euros, venez faire le choix!*" (I'm clearing the table for five euros, so come and make your choice.) We watched strawberries disappearing at warp speed when that call went out, and we stepped up for half a kilo ourselves.

WHEN IN PARIS,
DO AS THE PARISIANS

EVERYONE FEELS SOMEWHAT AWKWARD IN ANOTHER COUNTRY. IT'S NATURAL TO WATCH HOW THE NATIVES BEHAVE, AND TO copy their habits and mannerisms, even if unconsciously. Doing so helps us to blend in, and to feel more comfortable in what is, after all, a foreign environment. Here are some behaviors we've observed on the street, in shops, and in restaurants and have tried to incorporate into our behavior when we're in Paris.

Parisians always offer greetings when entering and leaving shops and restaurants, and shake hands when they meet. Women (and some men) kiss one cheek, then the other, and for very good friends a third time.

✦

We never see Parisians with maps in their hands, so they must have a copy of *Paris par arrondissement* at home. We explore our neighborhood on arrival, and put *l'Indispensable* in a pocket when we venture beyond.

✦

Parisians have radar that warns them of impending contact with persons, bicycles, dogs, and cars. They avoid each other with mere millimeters of separation. This takes practice, but it's a valuable skill.

✦

Paris is dressy: travelers stand out with their clothing, white jogging shoes, caps, and knapsacks. Emulate the locals; dress up a bit.

Nonsmoking sections in restaurants are now more common, but you still may be offered a non-smoking table next to smokers. It's pointless to complain. Rather than trying to reform the culture, try another restaurant.

✦

Parisians, like their countrymen and women, need bread with their food. It's positioned at the left-hand corner of the place setting, not always on its own plate.

✦

The European fashion with cutlery is to hold the fork upside down in the left hand and use the knife as a pusher. This practice can become habitual very quickly.

✦

There is much discussion about how Parisian women manage to keep their slim profiles while eating rich foods and drinking wine. We think the answer is that they eat well, but eat less.

✦

Parisians and the French generally keep their hands on the table, not in their laps, when at meals. Don't ask why, it's just the way it's done.

✦

French children are remarkably well behaved in restaurants. (Well-behaved dogs are welcome, too.) We esteem this behavior and wish our children had learned earlier in life to sit still and keep their voices down.

ABOUT OYSTERS

WE BELIEVE PROFOUNDLY THAT NOWHERE IN THE WORLD ARE MORE OYSTERS CONSUMED PER HEAD OF POPULATION THAN IN Paris. Some data support this position, though it would be hard to prove. Nevertheless, by our definition of a market as a place where you can find a lot of the same kind of thing at competitive prices, it would seem that Paris is a virtual marketplace for oysters, at least from September 1 to May 15.

A former editor of the Asian and European editions of *Time* magazine, Donald Morrison, wrote about oysters for the February 4/5, 2006, edition of the *Financial Times*. We have blended our own knowledge and experience with material shamelessly borrowed from his column, and from an article by Susan Herrmann Loomis in the Winter 2005-2006 issue (No. 76) of *France* magazine. They review facts that we like to recall when we're enjoying oysters during the cold months in Paris.

First to note is that oysters are widely available at the brasseries, cafés, and restaurants around the city and in the open markets. We are confident that they are fresh, having been rushed from the Atlantic coast (Normandy, Brittany, Arcachon Bay) and the Mediterranean by truck. Our evidence for this claim? We've never yet been made ill by an oyster eaten in Paris.

La Cargouille in the 15th arrondissement, and le Petit Celestin in the 4th, offer oysters whose grower is listed on the menu. Garnier, across from the Gare Saint-Lazare in the 8th, has a popular oyster bar, should you arrive early for your train. More than once we've feasted on oysters and a bottle of Sancerre at the Brasserie Lutétia, in front of the Hôtel Lutétia in the 6th arrondissement.

Second to note is the difference between two main types of oyster: *plat*, or flat, and *creuse*, or curved/crenellated. The flats are commonly called *belons*; they come from Brittany, where only about 1,500 tons a year are produced, of 130,000 tons of all oysters harvested. The most common and most popular *creuse* are called *fines de claires*; they are raised in ponds in Marennes-Oléron. *Fines de claires* are numbered 1 through 5 to distinguish the largest (#1) from the smallest (#5). A dozen #3s will set you back as much as a dozen euros in a restaurant, though much less in the open-air markets.

Only the flat oyster was produced in French waters until 1868, when a Portuguese vessel laden with oysters was trapped in the Gironde estuary by a storm. Thinking his cargo was spoiled, the captain ordered the whole lot dumped overboard. They thrived and became known as *Portugaises*. In the 1970s a disease wiped out nearly the entire population, resulting in the introduction of a hardy and disease-resistant oyster from Japan. The *Japonaise*, practically indistinguishable from the *Portugaise*, is now the main type of *creuse* found in the market.

Morrison observes that Charles de Gaulle's famous remark about the difficulty of governing a country of 300 cheeses could as easily have been made about oysters, of which there are some 246 different kinds. True aficionados will claim to have one or more favorites. Personally, we prefer the *belons*, which to us have greater delicacy and more of the flavor of the sea. But when it comes to oysters, to each his or her own.

Paris West Markets

8th and 16th arrondissements

ANTIQUE AND FLEA MARKETS

✦

COUR D'ANTIQUAIRES

54, rue Faubourg Saint-Honoré, 8th arr.

🚇 *Champs Elysées-Clemenceau*

Tuesday-Sunday 10 am-6 pm; some shops close from noon-2 pm or later

This collection of antique shops in a high-fashion street behind the Elysée Palace, the home of the French president, is worth more than a casual glance. The entrance is less inviting than one might expect, but eighteen sophisticated vendors offer a range of expensive furniture, art, and *objets décoratifs*.

HALLE D'AUTEUIL

13, rue Théophile Gautier, 16th arr. • 🚇 *Église d'Auteuil*

Tuesday-Sunday 10 am-6 pm; some shops close from noon-2 pm or later

A group of eight to ten antique shops surround a small tearoom and restaurant. Considering the upscale character of the neighborhood, treasure may lurk here undiscovered.

HÔTEL DUOUOT MONTAIGNE *See page 100*
15, avenue Montaigne, 8th arr.
Métro: Alma-Marceau
Viewing: daily 11 am-6 pm; Auctions: Monday-Friday 2-6 pm

COVERED FOOD MARKETS

✦

EUROPE
Rue Corvetto, 8th arr. • 🚇 *Villiers, Europe*
Tuesday-Saturday 8 am-1:30 pm, 4-7 pm; Sunday 8 am-1 pm

This little market is situated on the ground floor of a modern building that occupies a small city block. Long windows with rounded corners and the imaginative use of glass block give it the aspect of a ship at sea. Inside are half a dozen stands in a spotless environment. The *charcutier* offers a different *plat du jour* each day that local shoppers can take home and warm up for dinner.

PASSY
1, rue Bois le Vent, place Passy at rue Duban, 16th arr.
🚇 *La Muette*
Tuesday-Saturday, 8:30 am-1 pm, 4-7:30 pm; Sunday 8:30 am-1 pm

The anonymous concrete facade of this building may be off-putting, but a glass brick skylight and windows make the interior bright and airy. The Carioti family sells dried and fresh pastas, and raviolis stuffed with Gorgonzola, chopped ham, and other combinations. Le Boulanger du Marché has fresh-baked country-style breads from a wood-fired oven, including a five-grain loaf and a sunflower-seed variation known as *polka*.

SAINT-DIDIER

Rue Saint-Didier at rue Mesnil, 16th arr.

🚇 *Victor Hugo, Boissière*

Tuesday-Saturday 8:30 am-1 pm, 4-7:30 pm

Sunday 8:30 am-1 pm

From the outside this market looks like a reduced version of the Marché Secrétan, a mid-nineteenth century Baltard-style building. Inside, it is small and lacks any product or service of note. Outside on the rue Mesnil, a dozen open-air stands provide fresh meat, fish, poultry, and vegetables.

OPEN-AIR FOOD MARKETS

AGUESSEAU

Place de la Madeleine, 8th arr. • 🚇 *Concorde*

Tuesday, Friday 7 am-1:30 pm

The heart of Paris is poorly served by open markets, so this one is a surprise. Whether it is truly organic, as advertised by the city's department of markets, one can only determine by asking at each stand. The market, on the west side of the neoclassical Église de la Madeleine, is worth a visit if one is curious or needs to shop.

LECOURBE

Rue Lecourbe from rue Leblanc to rue Vasco de Gama, 15th arr.

🚇 *Balard* • *Wednesday 7 am-2:30 pm, Saturday 7 am-3 pm*

In this distant corner of the city, activity speeds up after midday to dispose of remaining produce. Vendors call out bargains, improving the terms as one o'clock approaches. One day we saw cantaloupe prices drop like rocks. At the last minute, shoppers stagger off with cartons of salad greens or tomatoes for the equivalent of a dollar or less.

LEFEVBRE

Boulevard Lefevbre from rue de Dantzig to rue Oliver de Serres, 15th arr.

🚇 *Porte de Versailles* • *Wednesday, 7 am-2:30 pm, Saturday, 7 am-3 pm*

Sidewalks are the most common location for small markets like this one. All the usual stalls are here to supply the neighborhood. At Le Callebasse, two African women sell unusual cocktail hors d'oeuvres.

SAINT-CHARLES

Rue Saint-Charles from rue de Javel to rue des Cévennes, 15th arr.

🚇 *Charles Michels* • *Tuesday, Friday, 7 am-2:30 pm*

Sycamores give some shade to this narrow, one-way street. The east side is given almost exclusively to food stalls, while the west side, from rue de la Convention to rue des Cévennes, is mostly clothing. We discover Sylvain Hordesseaux, whose seasonal rhubarb and asparagus are garden-fresh, along with carrots, onions, radishes, and other good things.

L'AMIRAL BRUIX

Boulevard de l'Amiral Bruix from rue Weber to rue Marbeau, 16th arr.

🚇 *Porte Maillot • Wednesday, 7 am-2:30 pm, Saturday 7 am-3 pm*

This small market does a local business at a leisurely pace, in a pretty setting in the northwest corner of the 16th arrondissement. Observed here: a poultry vendor, working behind a small screen, prepared a duckling for a customer by burning off the pinfeathers with a small gas torch.

AUTEUIL

Place Jean Lorrain, 16th arr.

🚇 *Michel Ange-Auteuil • Wednesday, 7 am-2:30 pm, Saturday 7 am-3 pm*

What a delight to arrive in this calm and airy setting beneath spreading sycamores. Everything one looks for in an open market is at its best here. Price markers are legible, and displays are arranged with consummate care and artistic flair. Above all, there is the smell and feel of freshness, of the best that France can produce or import to satisfy the world's most discriminating shopper, the French housewife.

GROS-LAFONTAINE

Rue Gros from rue Gautier to rue Fontaine,
rue Fontaine from rue Millet to rue de Boulainvilliers, 16th arr.

🚇 *Jasmin • Tuesday, Friday, 7 am-2:30 pm*

Where rue Gros intersects rue Fontaine, the street opens into the shady little Square du Pré aux Chevaux, or Horse Pasture Square. The market reflects the arrondissement in the high quality and fastidious displays.

Green beans poke up among lemons, and peppers sprout among tomatoes, in pleasing arrangements of texture and color. The fish seller presents four big lobsters, boiled to a rosy pink, in a silver bowl of chipped ice.

POINT DU JOUR

Avenue de Versailles from rue Gudin to rue le Marois, 16th arr.
🚇 *Porte de Saint-Cloud • Tuesday, Thursday, 7 am-2:30 pm*
Sunday 7 am-3 pm

It would be hard to find more flawless raspberries, melons at a more perfect pitch of ripeness, or more aromatic peaches than those of Jean-Marc Lechanteaux. Prices reflect what he has found a few hours before at the wholesale market in Rungis. The stand of Maison Lenoble in the little place Paul Raymond has the most beautiful display of vegetables we've ever seen. Radishes are piled to toppling heights in alternating rows of red and white. Spring onions are stacked in bunches, their stiff roots like little brooms; carrots are as clean as a surgeon's fingers.

PORTE MOLITOR

From place de la Porte Molitor on avenue General Sarrail
to boulevard Murat, 16th arr.
🚇 *Michel-Ange Molitor, Porte d'Auteuil*
Tuesday, Friday, 7 am-2:30 pm

Markets in the 16th arrondissement are for those who can afford the best. One stand sells raw silk coats; another, chic costume jewelry; a third, cans of truffled goose liver. The aroma of roasting chicken at F. Priolet tickles our noses. His prepared meats include pork loin stuffed with orange and kiwi, a shoulder of lamb anointed with herbed butter, a roast of veal filled with ground veal and chopped red bell peppers, and trimmed chops and brochettes ready to grill.

PRÉSIDENT WILSON *See page 105*
Avenue du Président Wilson from place d'Iéna to rue Debrousse, 16th arr.
🚇 *Iéna • Wednesday, 7am-2:30pm, Saturday, 7am-3pm*

MARKET STREET

RUE DE L'ANNONCIATION
Place de Passy to rue Raynouard, 16th arr.
🚇 *La Muette • Tuesday-Saturday 10 am-6 pm; Sunday morning*
A small street market cannot easily be charming and do its job, but this one handles both. A stone's throw in length, rue de l'Annonciation has all the necessary food shops plus a dry cleaner, a camera shop, a shoebox size tourist hotel, and two small restaurants—a wonderful neighborhood resource.

OTHER MARKETS

MARCHÉ AUX TIMBRES ET AUX CARTES TÉLÉPHONIQUES
See page 102
Avenue de Marigny from avenue Gabriel to allée Marcel Proust, 8th arr.
🚇 *Champs Elysées-Clemenceau*
Thursday, Saturday, Sunday, holidays 10 am-dusk

PARIS NORTH

9th, 10th, 17th, 18th and 19th arrondissements
La Gare du Nord, Montmartre, Clignancourt

MARKETPLACES

Marché Saint-Pierre · 122
Saint-Pierre Fabric Market

Marché aux Puces de Clignancourt · 126
Clignancourt Flea Market

Marché La Chapelle · 132
Covered Market

FOOD MARKETS

Marché Barbès · 134
Open-Air Market

Marché Saint-Quentin · 138
Covered Market

✦

Architect Victor Baltard · 141

Paris North Markets · 143

Marché Saint-Pierre

FABRIC MARKET

PLACE SAINT-PIERRE AT RUE LIVINGSTON, 18TH ARR.

BARBÈS-ROCHECHOUART

MONDAY–SATURDAY 9 AM–6 PM

TO REACH THIS UNUSUAL FABRIC MARKET, GET OFF THE MÉTRO AT THE BARBÉS-ROCHECHOUART ELEVATED STATION and go west along the north side of boulevard Rochechouart. Turn right on rue Clignancourt and take the first left on rue d'Orsel. You'll find yourself in a street of fabric shops that continues for three long blocks, ending in the place Saint-Pierre.

A number of specialty stores on rue d'Orsel stock buttons, braid, and fabric trimmings of all kinds. Village d'Orsel also carries ready-made

sheets, pillowcases, and bedcovers at bargain prices, as well as quality handbags, luggage, and leather goods. Moline, a large shop on the approach to place Saint-Pierre, has a huge inventory of fabrics as well as the hooks, buttons, fringes, bangles, and beads that decorators adore.

Le Marché Saint-Pierre is an old wooden building that houses five floors of fabrics of every imaginable color, texture, print, and weave. Le Marché Reine across the street is a competitor, but the prices, the variety, and the quality at Saint-Pierre make it worth the trip (*ça vaut le voyage*, as the French put it).

The sales program is superbly organized, and the goods are entic-

ing to judge by the number of shoppers and the intensity of commerce. Young salesmen in jeans and T-shirts carry the essential tools of their trade: a meter stick, a pair of scissors, a ballpoint pen, and a receipt book. They respond promptly, measure and rip off the proper length of the desired material, and fill out a payment form, which customers take to the cashier before collecting their purchases.

If we were furnishing a newly purchased apartment in Paris, we would come here for curtain and cushion materials. We saw big bolts of textured furniture coverings, some we would happily live with, others for different tastes. Mattress ticking and sheeting at several levels of quality suggest that a considerable fraction of Parisians still make their own bedding.

On the fourth floor we stumbled upon some wonderful cooks' aprons in various pleasing materials at €9 and €15; a selection of linen shopping bags at €12 and €14; and cotton bathrobes at €23. There is a large, comfortable sofa at every stair landing, where exhausted husbands catch a few winks while their spouses continue the quest.

The management does not discourage looking and touching. We watched shoppers who knew what they wanted and persevered until they found it. Admonitions such as *nous ne donnons pas d'échantillon* (we don't give samples) are stenciled prominently on the white painted rafters. Signs everywhere advise that every sale is final and that goods are non-returnable and non-exchangeable. Despite Draconian policies, the buzz of activity in this store tells us it is an impressive and appreciated resource.

Marché aux Puces de Clignancourt

EVERYONE HAS HEARD ABOUT THE ENORMOUS FLEA MARKET JUST OUTSIDE PARIS. THE FRENCH CALL IT LES PUCES DE Saint-Ouen, or les Puces de Clignancourt, referring to the Métro stop and *périphérique* entrance/exit here. This market is still to some extent a gathering of glorious junk from which one may glean gems, but over the years it has also become a straightforward antique market with specialists in every branch of the trade. A small *brocante* market, the Marché à la Ferraille, persists on rue Jean-Henry Fabre, which parallels the *périphérique*. There, a determined visitor can still find bargains.

On our first visit many years ago, Clignancourt was a dusty field with randomly parked trucks and wobbly trestle tables. Today it has sidewalks, food bars, and toilet facilities. Well-designed maps provide directions to fifteen different markets with more than three thousand stalls. Saturday and Sunday are the high traffic days in Clignancourt, while Monday is relatively quiet.

From the Porte de Clignancourt Métro station, walk under the *périphérique* (through a jam of hawkers and shell games) and turn left into rue des Rosiers, which connects with the entrances to nearly every one of the thirteen individual markets. There are half a dozen restaurants

here to which you may return later, exhausted and famished. Café Bert on rue Paul Bert is a classic of its kind, worth a stop for a coffee or a bite of lunch.

If you're seriously seeking something in a particular style or period, your visit will be more productive with a copy of *Tout Paris* or *Antique & Flea Markets of London & Paris* (see the bibliography) in hand. They will guide you to specialists in these markets. Knowing how items are categorized and priced requires detailed knowledge. If you plan to make expensive purchases, you might consider using a certified expert.

The enjoyment here is often more in the chase than in the capture, though once in a while you stumble on something wonderful that you never thought of looking for. Still, it takes a discriminating eye to note differences in quality, and careful study to compare similar objects in different stalls. There's also the issue of authenticity. We've bought a fair amount of Provençal furniture and learned that shelves and backs are often removed and used to make "new" antiques. So we're not surprised when the interior of a fine old armoire smells like the shoe polish that makes new wood look old.

On one visit we looked for ice-cream spoons. There were more variables than we had imagined, such as age, quality of the plate, number of items in the set, and state of preservation—not to mention the reputation of the maker. There were even spoons for right- or left-handed people. In the end, we found what we wanted at a price we were willing to pay.

Bargaining is less common in Clignancourt than in other flea markets, but we begin by asking for a 20 percent reduction. If we get 5 to 7 percent we feel satisfied. One can often get a better price by offering cash instead of a credit card. In any event, the door is usually open to a reasonable offer, and after some spirited and good-natured discussion, both sides can end up feeling pleased.

For a somewhat spooky experience—and if time is not a constraint—walk through Clignancourt during the week when all but a few stands are closed. One benefit is that you can better comprehend the organization and extent of this gigantic place; another is that you can see some of the most inspired graffiti in Paris.

Marché la Chapelle

COVERED MARKET

10, RUE DE L'OLIVE, 18TH ARR.

🚇 MARX DORMOY

TUESDAY-SATURDAY 8:30 AM-1 PM, 4-7:30 PM

SUNDAY 8:30 AM-1 PM

FOR STUDENTS OF ARCHITECTURE, THIS IS THE FINEST ORIGINAL COVERED MARKET STILL FUNCTIONING IN PARIS. Though not as old as Saint-Quentin or Beauvau, it is a splendid example of Victor Baltard's work (page 141) with its lacy iron structure, glass walls above the door level, and central clerestory. The exterior walls are covered with pale orange mortar, divided into large rectangles separated by iron framing. In an odd way, they give the building the look of a Japanese temple.

La Chapelle was constructed in 1858 as a way station for animals destined for the slaughterhouse at La Villette (now transformed into a park—see entry on the antiquarian and used book market, page 198). After the First World War it became a food market, and it was renovated in 1988.

Should you go out of your way to visit this remote location? It depends how you feel about seeing the best preserved of Paris's covered markets. A more convenient alternative might be the Carreau du Temple, an old covered market located in front of the Mairie (city hall) of the 3rd arrondissement. The building has not been maintained and is a bit sad, but its dimensions and use of materials tell what covered markets once were, both inside and out.

Thirty shops inside La Chapelle sell the same meat, cheese, fish, fruit, and vegetables that are staples in markets all over Paris, whether open-air or covered. This is an ordinary neighborhood, but regular clients demand and receive the freshest food at reasonable prices. And that, after all, is what these markets are for.

Marché Barbès

OPEN-AIR MARKET

BOULEVARD DE LA CHAPELLE FROM BOULEVARD BARBÈS TO
RUE DE TOMBUCTO, 18TH ARR.

🚇 BARBÈS-ROCHECHOUART

WEDNESDAY 7 AM-2:30 PM; SATURDAY 7 AM-3 PM

A VERITABLE SOUK, THIS NOISY, CROWDED FOOD MARKET IS PERMEATED WITH THE AROMAS OF FRESH MINT, CORI-ander, and parsley, the holy trinity of North African cuisine. Melons, oranges, and lemons are cut open to reveal ripe flesh. Stacks of eggplants and fresh bell peppers share space with red and yellow onions. We are transported to a medina in North Africa, surrounded by authentic faces and accents. Most vendors and shoppers are men wearing brimless, knitted caps, though we note a few women in black chadors with a child or two in tow.

The Métro thunders overhead, causing all voices to rise. Beggars and shady-looking characters offer clandestine merchandise, hissing urgently from narrow spaces between stalls. The crowd jostles and squeezes closer. Elbow to elbow, hip to hip, the market approaches a roaring climax at eleven o'clock. Our camera is viewed with suspicion, and it's almost impossible to get a clear shot of a stunning heap of cabbage heads, or a tottering mound of peppers.

Barbès is both challenging and fascinating. Vendors constantly call out their products: "*Tomates! Grenades! Oranges!*" and the prices of each.

We are amazed to see the roasting heads of lambs turning on spits. Tiny front teeth designed for clipping grass are glazed brown with juice, the eyeballs fire-blind. They suggest a lesson in comparative culture: chickens and turkey legs broiling on a spit in North Africa might look equally strange in that setting.

Saturday afternoon we stay to observe the cleanup. Big green trucks with crab-like pinchers push boxes and crates together, grasp them awkwardly, and deposit them in a compactor truck. City workers in green coveralls with green plastic brooms work quickly and efficiently, ignoring the women and children sorting through the leftovers.

As order is gradually restored, a water truck backs into the area and the hose tender drives before him a foaming broth of torn papers, broken melons, squashed peaches, and smelly heaps of ice left by the fish mongers. It surges into the gutters and toward the all-consuming sewers.

Marché Saint-Quentin

COVERED MARKET

BOULEVARD DE MAGENTA AT RUE DE CHABROL, 10TH ARR.

🚇 GARE DE L'EST

TUESDAY-SATURDAY 8:30 AM-1 PM, 4-7:30 PM;

SUNDAY 8:30 AM-1 PM

HISTORIANS TELL US THAT THE EARLIEST MARKETS EMERGED IN ANTIQUITY. WE IMAGINE PHILOSOPHERS AND statesmen strolling on the Stoa of Attalus, stepping into the Agora for a few purchases for their wives, and having a snack at a food stand. Covered markets in Europe appeared in the twelfth century, when the king awarded local lords the privilege of setting up markets. Louis VI, known as Le Gros, was the first to authorize markets in Paris.

In 1628 the first covered market in the city, les Enfants Rouge, was built on the site it occupies today at 39, rue de Bretagne. The market was scheduled for destruction in the 1980s, but an outcry from local residents saved it. A change of mayors in the 3rd arrondissement in the 1990s started the movement toward renovation and reopening in 1998. Sadly, its Baltard-style building did not survive.

Saint-Quentin is one of the best surviving covered markets in the Baltard style, designed by the architect Rabourdin. The large cast-iron and wood building is a must-see for lovers of architecture (along with the nearby church of Saint-Augustin). The ceiling soars forty feet overhead, and iron roof-trusses are set on cast-iron capitals with a Corinthian motif.

Glass walls beneath steel arches open grand vistas of the sky and the trees outside on the boulevard de Magenta, their leaves quaking gently in a morning breeze.

The clientele, like the neighborhood, is a slice of middle-class Paris. Locals shop here, and commuters stop on their way to and from the nearby Gare de l'Est. The market is clean, and the produce is first-rate, with beautifully arranged vegetable stands. In addition to the butcher shop there's a triperie and a kosher food stand. Services include a shoe repairman, a key shop, and the Bistro Saint-Quentin with coffee, croissants, and a few stronger things. As in other covered markets, miniature delivery trucks are parked here and there for the tots.

If your thoughts are turning toward a picnic, you can find what you need at the *traiteur* Daniel Verin. La Boutique de Tante Emma sells German foods, and some pretty blue china (teapots, serving dishes, cups, and mugs) by Wallendorfer. For jams and jellies, stop at La Ferme Saint-Quentin, and if houseplants are on your list, Un Amour de Fleur at the main entrance is the place.

ARCHITECT VICTOR BALTARD

THE FACE OF PARIS IN THE NINETEENTH CENTURY WAS CHANGED BY SEVERAL MEN, OF WHOM THE BEST KNOWN IS Eugène Haussman, the planner of the grand boulevards, parks, and squares that define the modern city. Another was one of Haussman's closest friends and associates, Victor Baltard (1805-1874), who had much to do with the way Paris looked and worked then as now.

The son of Louis-Pierre Baltard, a renowned architect, artist, and member of the faculty of the École des Beaux Arts, Victor distinguished himself early in life by submitting the winning design for the tomb of Napoléon I. He was denied the commission because, at thirty-six, he was considered too young and inexperienced. He entered the government architectural service and rose rapidly, partly as a result of his friendship with Haussman, to become chief architect of the city of Paris. In this capacity he designed the city hall, which burned down in 1871.

Baltard's best-known work was Les Halles (the central food market that was moved to Rungis, page 210). The initial design had poor traffic patterns and bad ventilation. After a personal visit by Napoléon III, construction was halted. Working with his colleague Félix-Emmanuel Callet, Baltard improved the design, and the first of ten buildings was completed in 1853. His great innovation was a glass and iron umbrella-shaped roof that maximized natural light and ventilation. This style was later used in the construction of covered neighborhood markets, of which Saint-Quentin, Saint-Martin, and La Chapelle still exist.

In addition to Les Halles, Baltard designed the church of Saint-

Augustin, on the boulevard Malesherbes. It was the first time that an iron frame was used inside a French church as a decorative as well as structural feature. By the end of a long and celebrated career he had become, like his father, a professor of architectural theory at the École des Beaux Arts. Published widely and acclaimed for his work, Baltard became an Officer of the Legion of Honor and was elected to the Institut de France.

Paris North Markets

9th, 10th, 17th, 18th, and 19th arrondissements

ART, ANTIQUE, AND FLEA MARKETS

✦

MARCHÉ AUX PUCES DE CLIGNANCOURT *See page 126*

Saint-Ouen, adjacent to the 18th arr. • 🚇 *Porte de Clignancourt*

Saturday, Sunday, Monday 7 am-7:30 pm

COVERED FOOD MARKETS

✦

BATIGNOLLES

96bis, rue Lemercier, 17th arr. • 🚇 *Brochant, Fourche*

Tuesday-Saturday 8:30 am-1 pm, 4-7:30 pm; Sunday 8 am-1 pm

Batignolles has suffered the fate of several other covered markets. Its Baltard-style building was replaced in 1979 by an ugly concrete structure whose ground floor serves as a market. Nevertheless, the sellers are friendly and accommodating. An advertisement for free-range Brittany hogs catches our eye: "*Chez nous, être cochon c'est naturel,*" which we translate as "With us, being a pig is natural."

LA CHAPELLE *See page 132*

Rue de l'Olive, 18th arr. • 🚇 *Marx Dormoy*

Tuesday-Saturday 8 am-1 pm, 4-7:30 pm; Sunday 8 am-1 pm

SAINT-MARTIN

31-33, rue du Château d'Eau at rue Bouchardon, 10th arr.

🚇 *Château d'Eau, Jacques Bensergent*

Tuesday-Saturday 8:30 am-1 pm, 4-7:30 pm; Sunday 8:30 am-1 pm

In front of a modern building, the stone portals of the old market were re-erected as a symbol of the vanished past. Half a dozen stands provide meat, fish, cheese, fruit, and vegetables. A small restaurant is accessible from the sidewalk and from inside the market, and a good flower shop shares space and access. The organization that oversees covered markets, Marchés Couverts de Paris, has offices upstairs.

SAINT-QUENTIN *See page 138*

See page 138

Boulevard de Magenta at rue de Chabrol, 10th arr. • 🚇 *Gare de l'Est*

Tuesday-Saturday 8:30 am-1 pm, 4-7:30 pm; Sunday 8:30 am-1 pm

SECRÉTAN

33, rue Secrétan, 19th arr. • 🚇 *Simon -Bolivar*

Tuesday-Thursday, 8:30 am-7:30 pm; Friday-Saturday, 8:30 am-8 pm

Sunday 8 am-2 pm

Some of these brick and iron Baltard-style structures have disappeared (see La Chapelle, Saint-Didier, and Saint- Quentin). They have a soaring elegance that will be hard to give up if modernization sweeps them away. Local residents have saved this one; Secrétan has been declared a protected site.

TERNES

8 bis, rue Lebon, in the block bounded by rue Toricelli, rue Faraday,
rue Lebon, and rue Bayen, 17th arr. • 🚇 *Ternes*
Tuesday-Saturday, 8:30 am-1 pm, 4-7:30 pm; Sunday, 8:30 am-1 pm

The Baltard-style 1852 market pavilion was torn down, to re-emerge in
1970 in a radically different form. Were it not for the yellow and green
sign hanging over the entrance, you might miss the market entirely. A
dry-cleaning and clothing repair shop are featured. The flowers, fish, and
cheese look and smell splendid, and there is plenty to choose from. A
small bakery is a pleasant addition, and the coffee shop features a variety
of fresh grinds and a selection of loose teas.

OPEN-AIR FOOD MARKETS

✦

ALIBERT

Rue Alibert from rue Claude Vellefaux to rue Bichat, 10th arr.
🚇 *Goncourt* • *Sunday, 7am-3pm*

A tiny market along a narrow sidewalk with scarcely room to maneu-
ver, this would be worth a visit for those staying in the neighborhood.
Two vegetable vendors, a butcher, and a flower stall make up the regular
stands, plus a mattress-seller who also re-canes chairs.

BATIGNOLLES

*Boulevard des Batignolles from rue des Batignolles to
rue Boursault, 17th arr.* • 🚊 *Rome, Place de Clichy
Saturday, 9 am-2 pm*

Batignolles was the first *biologique* (organic) food market in Paris, leading
to the establishment of a Sunday organic market on boulevard Raspail,
and others in place Madeleine and place Brancusi. It draws a lively crowd
of shoppers for whom organic produce is effectively a religion.

BERTHIER

*Boulevard de Reims from rue du Marquis d'Arlandes to
rue de Senlis, 17th arr.* • 🚊 *Porte de Champerret
Wednesday 7 am-2:30 pm, Saturday 7 am-3 pm*

A small, pleasant neighborhood market at the very edge of the périphérique has standard offerings of meat, fish, poultry, fruit, vegetables, and
cheese.

NAVIER

Rue Navier behind the church of Saint-Joseph des Epinettes, 17th arr.
🚊 *Porte de Saint-Ouen* • *Tuesday, Friday 7 am-2:30 pm*

This is a quiet neighborhood of small apartment buildings. Across the
street from the tiny market the local restaurant-bar, La Pétanque, seems
so have been lifted from a village in rural France. The market and the
bar, along with the nearby school and the cemetery, identify the bound-
aries of French life.

BARBÈS *See page 134*
Boulevard de la Chapelle from boulevard Barbès to
rue de Tombucto, 18th arr. • 🚇 *Barbès-Rochechouart*
Wednesday 7 am-2:30 pm, Saturday 7 am-3 pm

ORDENER
Rue Ordener from rue Montcalm to rue Championnet, 18th arr.
🚇 *Guy Moquet, Jules Joffrin*
Wednesday 7am-2:30pm, Saturday 7am-3pm

The market is on a narrow sidewalk, so shoppers are squeezed between the stalls and the shops, most of which stay open on market days. One of our favorite *charcuteries*, Joelle et Elivette, is here, as well as Atlan, a fruit and vegetable stand with a good selection and competitive prices.

ORNANO
Boulevard Ornano from rue du Mont Cenis to rue Ordener, 18th arr.
🚇 *Simplon* • *Tuesday, Friday 7 am-2:30 pm, Sunday 7 am-3 pm*

A short walk from the city hall and the rue Duhesme street market, the Ornano open market seems quite different in character and clientele. Most sellers and buyers are North African, and the goods reflect their tastes: heaps of dried spices, bunches of fresh mint, and cheap cuts of lamb and kid.

CRIMÉE-CURIAL

Rue de Crimée at rue de Curial, 19th arr. • 🚇 *Crimée*

Tuesday, Friday, 7 am-2:30 pm

Along with the big Francprix supermarket on the corner, a tiny market of half a dozen stands loyally serves its neighborhood, but neither is of serious interest to the traveler.

PLACE DES FÊTES

Place des Fêtes, 19th arr. • 🚇 *Place des Fêtes*

Tuesday, Friday 7 am-2:30 pm, Sunday 7 am-3 pm

One of the largest markets far from the center of Paris, the convenience of the Métro makes a point in its favor, and most of the food stalls offer fresh meat, fish, and produce as good as we found elsewhere. But even a children's playground in the center of this huge open square does not offset the depressing effect of anonymous apartment buildings and stores around the perimeter. At the north end of the market, a number of stalls sell fabrics, clothing, mattresses, and some furniture.

JEAN-JAURÈS

Avenue Jean-Jaurès from rue de l'Ourcq to rue des Ardennes, 19th arr.

🚇 *Ourcq* • *Tuesday, Thursday, 7 am-2:30 pm, Sunday 7 am-3 pm*

An excellent small market serves this working-class part of Paris, with every kind of fresh meat, fish, cheese, and produce at reasonable prices. Vendors are little concerned with beautiful displays for shoppers or travelers, but the atmosphere is friendly and businesslike.

Place de Joinville and rue Jomard, behind the church of
Saint-Jacques and Saint-Christophe, 19th arr.

🚇 *Crimée* • *Tuesday 7 am-2:30 pm, Sunday 7 am-3 pm*

In the small square behind the church, the voices of shoppers pleading
or demanding, of sellers calling or complaining, blend into a surge of
sound that is amplified by the close proximity of buildings and the ethnic
diversity of the shoppers. Early in the morning there is an opportunity
to observe towers of radishes, peppers, tomatoes, and eggplants before
shoppers reduce them to rubble. Potatoes and onions by the sack go so
fast that fresh supplies must be rushed from trucks along the Canal de
l'Ourcq, where tourist boats chug toward the Parc de la Villette.

PORTE BRUNET

Avenue de la Porte Brunet from boulevard Sérrurier to
boulevard d'Indochine/boulevard d'Algérie, 19th arr.

🚇 *Danube* • *Wednesday 7 am-2:30 pm, Saturday 7 am-3 pm*

Coming up from the Métro into the lovely little place de Rhin et Danube
is like entering another world: quiet streets, small brick houses, low-
profile apartment buildings, and grand old sycamore trees. On rue du
Général Brunet, wide sidewalks offer room for shoppers, gossipers, kids
on roller skates or skateboards, and a panhandler or two. This pleasant
place also has a classic collection of neighborhood food shops.

PORTE D'AUBERVILLIERS

Avenue d'Aubervilliers, 19th arr. • 🚇 *Porte de la Chapelle*
Wednesday 7 am-2:30 pm, Saturday 7 am-3 pm

This tiny market in a neighborhood of bleak brick apartments can vary from a single vegetable stand on a cold, rainy day to a dozen diverse stalls in good weather. The site on the northern edge of Paris is not pretty, but the people who live here want fresh food, and this is where they get it.

VILLETTE

Boulevard de la Villette from rue Bornouf to rue Rébeval, 19th arr.
🚇 *Belleville* • *Wednesday 7 am-2:30 pm, Saturday 7 am-3 pm*

Essentially, this market is an extension of the Marché Belleville. It is held Tuesday and Friday on the same median plaza, south of the Belleville Métro station. Old sycamores make it more pleasant to shop than the treeless upper part of the neighboring Belleville market.

MARKET STREETS

✦

RUE CADET

From rue de Provence to rue la Fayette, 9th arr. • 🚇 *Cadet*
Tuesday-Saturday 10 am-6 pm; Sunday morning

This narrow street with tall buildings on both sides at first seems dark and forbidding, but on closer examination becomes a friendly shopping street. A small *confiserie-épicerie*, A La Mère de Famille, was founded here in 1761, a date proudly displayed above the second-floor windows.

RUE LÉVIS

From rue Legendre to place P. Goubaux, 17th arr. • 🚇 *Villiers*
Tuesday-Saturday 10 am-6 pm; Sunday morning

A long pedestrian street, rue de Lévis offers a mixture of food, clothing, flowers, and services. Though not particularly colorful, it serves its neighborhood with a full complement of specialized shops and two big Monoprix markets.

RUE PONCELET

From avenue des Ternes to rue Bayen, 17th arr. • 🚇 *Place des Ternes*
Tuesday-Saturday 10 am-6 pm; Sunday morning

A few blocks west of place des Ternes, this fine neighborhood market sits on the angle formed by rue Bayen and rue Poncelet. The big shop at the corner, Boucheries Roger, forms the hinge. There are good fishmongers and produce stands in both streets. Two stübli in rue Poncelet advertise German-Austrian pastries and East European specialties.

RUE DEJEAN

From rue Poulet to rue des Poissonniers, 18th arr. • 🚇 *Chateau Rouge*
Tuesday-Saturday 10 am-6 pm; Sunday morning

This short street behind the Gare du Nord is in an African neighborhood. The butcher shops feature inexpensive cuts of kid and mutton, and the produce stands have more than the ordinary percentage of bruised vegetables. Most shoppers are looking for bargains, and there is a good-natured hubbub throughout the day. As the closing hour approaches, remainders are hawked at rock-bottom prices.

RUE DU POTEAU/DUHESME

Rue du Poteau at place Charles Bernard to rue Ordener, 18th arr.

🚇 *Jules Joffrin • Tuesday-Saturday 10 am-6 pm; Sunday morning*

In the rue du Poteau look for Maistre Guillaume, who spit-roasts everything in huge brick ovens: whole chickens, turkey thighs, quail, ducks, rabbits, spare ribs, and boned turkey roasts stuffed with prunes or chestnuts, or wrapped with bacon. White-coated employees pull off the roasted ribs, joints, or birds, and put them into foil-lined paper bags with a little juice. Farther on, the tiny rue Duhesme, no more than ten shop-fronts in length, packs in all the essential goods and services of a typical market street. Fine vegetables are well displayed, along with fresh and diverse offerings of fish and shellfish, a neat, clean butcher shop, a proper bakery, and a *charcuterie.*

OTHER MARKETS

❖

MARCHÉ SAINT-PIERRE *See page 122*

Place Saint-Pierre at rue Livingston, 18th arr. • 🚇 Barbès-Rochechouart
Monday-Saturday 9 am-6 pm

PARIS EAST

11th, 12th, and 20th arrondissements
La Bastille, Pére Lachaise, La Porte de Montreuil

MARKETPLACES

Marché aux Vieux Papiers · 156
Old Papers Market

Marché aux Puces de Montreuil · 160
Porte de Montreuil Flea Market

Viaduc des Artisans · 164
Viaduct Art and Craft Shops

FOOD MARKETS

Marché Bastille · 170
Open-Air Market

Rue d'Aligre · 176
Market Street

Marché Beauvau · 180
Covered Market

✦

Le Baron Rouge · 182

Paris East Markets · 183

Marché aux Vieux Papiers

OLD PAPERS MARKET

AVENUE GALLIÉNI FROM RUE DU COMMANDANT
HERMINIER TO AVENUE JOFFRE, PORT DE VINCENNES,
ADJACENT TO THE 20TH ARR.

🚊 SAINT-MAND-TOURELLE

WEDNESDAY 9 AM-6 PM

THIS MARKET IS NOT, STRICTLY SPEAKING, IN PARIS, BUT OF PARIS. IT'S A FASCINATING PLACE TO STROLL DOWN FRANCE'S memory lane, and to shop for small, esoteric collectibles that are impossible to find elsewhere. Many French people come here to look for a postcard mailed from their native village. Tens of thousands of used cards are indexed geographically for France and its overseas dependencies or by subject matter, while foreign cards are filed by country of origin.

Usually the boxes of cards are turned so that clients cannot riffle through them but must ask for what they want. The dealer determines whether it's available, then hands over a selection for review. If you prefer to look for yourself, you must specify an interest. Some boxes are arranged by rubrics such as sports and leisure activities, and turned so browsing clients can serve themselves. The price of a card averages €1 to €2, but rare items may cost €25 or more.

Beyond the postcard collections that make up the core of this market, there is an amazing variety of small things, most made of paper, which some collectors value. For example: bar coasters (known as *sous-bock*),

63 T...NECTAIRE
63 CL...CHATEAU...
62 Puy de Dôme BERT
62 WIMEREUX
62 le TOUQUET
62 ...PAL
62 LENS
62 CALAIS
...BOU...
ARRAS
...aus Va...
...au S.T
...PQR
...ais N.N.C

62 Pas de Calais G.H
62 P de Calais E.F
62 P de Calais C
62 P de Calais B
62 Pas de Calais A
61 Bas...
61 ORNÉ
SENLIS
60. PIERREFONDS.
CREPY en VALOIS
CREIL
60. COYE LA FORET
COMPIÈGNE
Beauvais

matchboxes, small colored cards with religious homilies (*chromos*), old letters, comic books, movie posters, paperback books, magazines, matchbook-covers, thirty-three and forty-five rpm record covers, and more. If you're interested in French detective novels and spy thrillers, you can probably fill out your holdings of any author.

There is a tendency here to slip into flea market goods. We found CDs and DVDs, telephone cards, caps from Champagne corks, brooches, key rings, foreign coins, and even old Barbie and G.I. Joe dolls. There are military medals, whole armies of miniature soldiers, and peculiar little ceramic figurines called *feves*, made to resemble the three magi. Traditionally, *feve* (fava) beans were baked into a cake served the twelfth night after Christmas. The person in whose slice the *feve* was found became king or queen for a day. Now tiny magi have replaced the *feve* bean.

After postcards, the largest type of paper collectible is trading cards. Most relate to U.S. sports teams, but there is an impressive variety of other subjects, such as rock music, history, and film. Europeans avidly trade soccer and rugby cards, 90 percent of which are manufactured in and distributed from the United States. After a morning in this market, we went away puzzled and amazed at what people value and covet.

Marché aux Puces de Montreuil

PORTE DE MONTREUIL FLEA MARKET

AVENUE DE PROFESSEUR ANDRÉ LEMIERRE AT PLACE DE LA
PORTE DE MONTREUIL, 20TH ARR.

🚇 PORTE DE MONTREUIL

SATURDAY-MONDAY 7 AM-7:30 PM

FROM THE SUBWAY EXIT, CROSS THE BRIDGE OVER THE PÉRIPHÉRIQUE AND ENTER A MARKET SO VAST AND crowded it's almost impossible to cover in an hour. As you approach, smooth-talking young men with collapsible tables may be scattered around the place de Montreuil, tempting the crowd with a game of chance. The idea is to guess, after a series of deft moves, which of three cards will show up in the left, right, and center positions. We saw a lot of money changing hands here.

The rush of traffic on the *périphérique* and the jam in the aisles make this market a tumultuous experience. You can buy what look like new goods in shrink-wrapped cartons. A few stands offer the lamps, glassware, table settings, and household bric-a-brac (*brocante*) that are standard flea market fare. But the main focus of this market is hardware, a vast proliferation of goods such as electric drills, sanding machines, wrench sets, and toolboxes that are sold at shockingly low prices. More than that; everything for the fully supplied kitchen is here, mostly new, as well as commercial and home hardware.

You might come to Montreuil to look for a wristwatch a clock-

radio, a professional sausage-slicer, a hair dryer, or electric wall switches; or perhaps you're shopping for soap, toothbrushes, and hand and body lotion. It's all here, but remember the rule: caveat emptor.

There is a large selection of replacement parts for cars. We once searched this market to replace a broken rear-view mirror for the Saab we had bought in Switzerland. As things turned out, we found all the head-lights, taillights, windshield wipers, and fog lamps we could imagine, but our particular quest was unsuccessful.

Bed linen is available, along with bolts of yard goods. There are mounds of clothing that buyers must paw through to find what they want: shirts, underwear, and socks make up the bulk of it. We looked at running shoes and leather shoes, hats and scarves, skirts and sweaters, down jackets and leather jackets, along with a proliferation of blouses and trousers too great to describe. There's even a touch of fashion: stylish hats, handbags, and luggage.

On Ascension Day and Toussaint, an event called a *grand déballage* (a big unpacking) brings in a flood of dealers, shoppers, and gawkers like us. Should you own property in Paris, this might be the place to outfit it, though it would be advisable to send someone familiar with the market to make the actual selections.

There is a rough edge in this market that, while not threatening, is still a bit off-putting. Montreuil is different from the Vanves flea market, and may be of less interest to the casual visitor. Nevertheless it has a flavor and grit that make it worth seeing.

Viaduc des Artisans

AVENUE LEDRU-ROLLIN TO RUE DE CHARENTON, 12TH ARR.

🚇 GARE DE LYON

TUESDAY-SATURDAY 10 AM-6 PM;

some shops close from noon to 2 pm or later

AN INTELLIGENT AND AESTHETICALLY PLEASING RESTORATION OF AN ABANDONED RAILROAD VIADUCT WAS COMPLETED in 1998 as a joint effort of the city of Paris and the government of the 12th arrondissement. It has brought many benefits to residents and businesses in the neighborhood. Some values have been sacrificed, such as low-rent housing, but the restoration has given a needed face-lift and an economic boost to a tired part of Paris.

Fifty-six arched spaces house a variety of shops and services devoted to the decorative arts and home design. Some are studios where visitors can watch artists at work, and where original furniture, lace, and gold-embossed leather-covered books are for sale. Espace Chevalier caught our eye with cushions made from Kilim carpets, as well as rugs, tapestries, and fabrics. Le Bonheur des Dames is sure to please, with an assortment of linens, plus bangles and beads to dress up a garment or a piece of furniture. Mahia Kent weaves scarves, jackets, and coats on her large and impressive hand loom.

N'Omades Authentiques offers strange and beautiful decorative objects from Asia. Cécile et Jeanne have created some of the most striking costume jewelry we have seen in Paris. Michel Pintad has original lamps, and Expositions Contemporaines features novel ceramics.

Finally, take a look at the unusual handmade jewelry and picture frames at Atelier de Talec, or fabric flowers for fashion and decoration by Guillet (in Paris since 1896). The most original item we saw was at Zephyr; holographic images are captured in blocks of optical glass. These artisans can present a photo of a child or loved one in a way that is extraordinarily realistic and even a bit spooky.

The last section of the viaduct, from rue Rambouillet to the Jardin de Reuilly, is occupied by a sports shop and by Surcouf, a large computer/accessory store. For coffee, tea, or a bite of lunch, stop at the Café Arrosoir at boulevard Diderot or Le Viaduc Café at rue Abel. Both offer reliable bistro dishes and outdoor seating in good weather.

A striking feature of the Viaduc is the pedestrian walkway atop the old right-of-way. It begins behind the new opera house at place Bastille

and ends in the Jardin de Reuilly about a mile away. Both sides of the path are thickly planted with bamboo, pyracantha, roses, and viburnum. There are bridges, benches, fountains, convenient stairways to the street, and an elevator for the handicapped.

Some small, private niches set back from the path with a southern exposure are enticing on a sunny day. Young locust (robinia) trees have fulfilled their promise and grown large and leafy; climbing roses are more than halfway up their trellises. This is one of the best maintained public gardens in Paris, among the loveliest and most soothing experiences in this busy city.

If you prefer old-fashioned charm, the Viaduc is not the market for you. But if you're looking for contemporary French craftsmanship, a visit to the Viaduc des Artisans, including a bistro lunch and a wonderful digestive walk afterward, is a rewarding way to pass an afternoon.

Marché Bastille

(FORMERLY RICHARD LENOIR) OPEN-AIR MARKET

BOULEVARD RICHARD LENOIR FROM RUE AMELOT
TO RUE SAINT-SABIN, 11TH ARR.

🚇 BASTILLE

THURSDAY 7 AM-2:30 PM; SUNDAY 7 AM-3 PM

THE BASTILLE MARKET IS ONE OF THE LARGEST OPEN FOOD MARKETS IN PARIS, AND PERHAPS THE MOST DEMOCRATIC. It reflects in some way the history of this place, where in the initial and

defining moment of the French Revolution in 1789 an enraged citizenry tore down the detested prison that stood there. Today, men and women of every age and race shop here. Children scramble underfoot, and foreigners with backpacks look curiously at the merchandise and the people.

Three broad alleys of stalls stretch four long city blocks. Park-like areas with flat fountains of white marble and small plantings interrupt the commerce. The fountains provide a space to pause

and chat. Children paddle their feet in the water, and beggars kneel with hands cupped in supplication. The sidewalks are lined with plane trees and the plaza is adorned with a double row of acacias, so the whole area is cool and pleasant on hot summer days. Ornate cast-iron street lamps give the market a vaguely Victorian aspect, but the throb of business has a definitely contemporary feeling.

In the past few years, the south end of the market, nearest place Bastille, has been infiltrated by a profusion of stands selling jewelry, handbags, and inexpensive clothing, mainly for young people. It's busy, colorful, and the music is upbeat. Perhaps changes like this will bring the new generation needed to keep the open markets thriving.

On one visit, we watched an elderly gentleman purchase a crab. Not satisfied with what he was offered, he handed it back to the vendor and asked for a male instead of a female (we were surprised that females were for sale). The vendor took a quick look and complied. The old gentleman smiled and paid, pleased that he knew as much as the vendor.

In the fall, there is a profusion of game, and the wild mushrooms are utterly compelling: *cèpes* as big as our hands, like those we've hunted on the mountain slopes of Provence, and oyster mushrooms whose aroma tells you how they got their name. In every season, produce vendors have unusual things, such as the thistlelike cardoon, a relative of the artichoke. Every fresh herb imaginable is sold here—dried bunches remind us of shaving brushes.

This Sunday morning, a girl with orange hair and two guys in jeans and cowboy boots are playing country-western music on guitar, banjo, and saxophone. Despite the paucity of coins in the cap on the ground in front of them, they keep up the beat. This is a popular place for music groups. There's plenty of room to perform, and in a busy market, persistence will ultimately bring enough contributions for a hearty lunch and a carafe of *vin ordinaire*.

In addition to food, clothing of all kinds and all price levels is stacked, draped, and hung about. We found the biggest hardware selection we've seen at any open market. The scissors salesman shouted rhythmically, "Straight from the factory, come and try them, cut with them, take advantage this MORN-ing!" It's a shopping opportunity for everyone who knows how to enjoy it, and judging by the crowds they are taking full advantage.

Rue d'Aligre

Note: as of June 2006 rue d'Aligre was being repaved and the market was moved to place d'Aligre. When this project is completed, the situation will return to that described below.

EVERY DAY BUT MONDAY ON THE RUE D'ALIGRE, A FANTAS-TIC MEDLEY OF PEOPLE, PRODUCTS, AND FOOD MAGICALLY appears, then disappears by early afternoon. For the brief time between, one can experience an authentic bazaar with the reputation of being one of the best of all the Paris street markets. The area actually combines three different markets; the Beauvau covered market in place d'Aligre, the flea market on the west side of place d'Aligre, and the street market.

This is one of the most popular places for tourists, and foreign dress and accents confirm that the guidebooks are being read. If the merchants sometimes seem a bit impatient, it may be due to the presence of a high proportion of onlookers relative to shoppers. When you stop to take a picture, don't be surprised if this fast-moving, boisterous crowd bumps you around, so keep a sharp eye and practice your avoidance skills.

Hard bargaining goes along with rock-bottom prices. But you've got to be on your toes: commerce is quick, and the vendors won't coddle

you. North Africans, who work hard for a sale, operate most of the street stands. Regular shops located behind the stands supply routine needs. The flower stand seems to have an unlimited selection at popular prices; roses are sold in bunches stacked like cordwood.

Milling crowds of shoppers are eager to see everything and buy the best, and mothers with collapsible strollers are intent on shopping and keeping track of their children at the same time. Merchants shout their wares, which is often how you learn of a bargain that otherwise would be ignored in the crush.

The main concentration of vegetable, fruit, and meat stands is at the north end of the street, from place d'Aligre to rue Crozatier. South of place d'Aligre, clothing stands take their place. No fancy outfits here, but simple cotton shirts, skirts, trousers, and jackets, along with inexpensive shoes, boots, and purses. Yet everyone seems to find satisfaction in the rue d'Aligre, which is doubtless the reason for its reputation.

As 2 pm approaches, merchants start taking down their stands while lowering the price of remaining produce, happier to sell it cheap than to cart it home. Crisp heads of red-leaf and oak-leaf lettuce that were going earlier for about €1 each come down until finally a whole case goes for €3 or €4. If you don't mind the frenzy, it can be worth the wait.

Precisely at 2:30, green-clad foot soldiers move down the sidewalks and deploy plastic brooms made to resemble bound branches. Streams of water cascade through the street, scattering the last of the shoppers and a few women picking through the remains. Soon the trash is swept into heaps, shoveled into trucks, and only the damp street steaming quietly in the sun shows that there was a market here at all.

Marché Beauvau

COVERED MARKET

PLACE D'ALIGRE, 12TH ARR.

🚇 LEDRU-ROLLIN

TUESDAY-SUNDAY 7:30 AM-12:30 PM

THIS MARKET HAS CHANGED LITTLE IN TWO HUNDRED YEARS. BEAUVAU IS THE SECOND OLDEST COVERED MARKET (after Enfants Rouges) but one of the most striking. It is registered by the government as a historic site and therefore is protected from demolition or alteration. The massive roof is supported on huge limestone columns, and the feeling inside of light and space is accentuated by a complex puzzle of gray-painted wooden roof beams.

The central fountain is no mere decoration, but a practical, cast-iron monolith that supplies merchants and cleaning crews with washing water. Grooves chiseled in the immense, worn stones, where generations of Parisians have trod, carry off dirt and debris with the washing water when the market closes. Small specialty stands for meat, cheese, and produce, are arranged in a grid, which makes it easy to get around and disperses the crowd.

Even if you have no food shopping to do, this market is worth visiting as a model of covered markets in Paris, illustrating how they functioned before the introduction of the open-air markets. The spaciousness, the sense of leisure, and the orderliness of the experience all attest to what food shopping was traditionally, and perhaps also shows how the generations pass on appropriate behaviors.

One stand we particularly like is Angellilo, where you can buy every kind of dressed poultry, including fresh *magret* (duck breast), and turkey parts, which are somewhat unusual. A shop just inside the doorway from place d'Aligre stocks Italian specialties, including every imaginable kind of pasta, paper-thin slices of *prosciutto di Parma*, and hard chunks of authentic Parmesan cheese.

We have not often seen the slabs of dried codfish from which one of our favorite dishes, *brandade de morue*, is made, but they are sold at a small stand on the opposite side of the market. The beer seller here carries the delightful name Delirium Tremens, and offers nine different kinds of tapenades, plus an *anchoide*, a *harissa*, and a variety of olives.

Beauvau is an oasis of calm compared with the tumult in the rue d'Aligre outside. People form queues, and the vendors take their time with each client, as if he or she were king or queen for five minutes. You have to be patient, but when you finally reach the head of the line you enjoy their full attention, along with a smile and an exchange of gossip.

LE BARON ROUGE

1, rue Théophile Rossel, 12th arr.

🚇 *Ledru-Rollin • Tuesday-Sunday, 10 am-6 pm*

This wine bar and bistro with nine yards of character is located behind the covered Beauvau market, just off place d'Aligre. It's a source of wine *en vrac*, that is, from the barrel, which buyers carry away in their own bottles or in a plastic container called a *cubitainer*. This colorful place has the cracked tile floors, mustard-colored walls, and ancient zinc bar that virtually define the word *bistro*. A dozen different red and white wines are available for tasting. Small, charming, down-at-the-heel, legitimate—Le Baron is all these things and more. Get a glass of Sancerre or Beaujolais to go with your veal sausage and pan-roasted potatoes (as only the French know how to make them), and for a while you'll stop thinking about restaurants with Michelin stars.

On weekend mornings during the season, a truck pulls up to the curb with oysters from Brittany, and soon the feasting begins, spilling out into the street and along the sidewalk in both directions. For €5 or €6 you get half a dozen shucked oysters and a basket of brown bread and butter. Buy a glass of wine at the bar inside and find a place to eat at one of the barrels on the sidewalk, or on the hood of a parked car. There is likely to be a brass band, singing, dancing in the street, and general merriment. It's an experience not to be missed.

Paris East Markets

11th, 12th, and 20th arrondissements

ART, ANTIQUE, AND FLEA MARKETS

✦

MARCHÉ AUX PUCES D'ALIGRE

Place d'Aligre, 12th arr. • 🚇 *Ledru-Rollin*

Tuesday-Sunday 8 am-1 pm

The smallest of the Paris flea markets, this one occupies half of the place d'Aligre, across from the Beauvau covered market. One can see a great deal of inexpensive *brocante* in half an hour's stroll.

MARCHÉ AUX PUCES DE MONTREUIL *See page 160*

*Avenue de Professeur André Lemierre at place de la
Porte de Montreuil, 20th arr.*

🚇 *Porte de Montreuil* • *Saturday-Monday 7 am-7:30 pm*

MARCHÉ AUX VIEUX PAPIERS *See page 156*

*Porte de Vincennes, north side of avenue Galliéni, rue du Commandant
Herminier to avenue Joffre, outside 20th arr.*

🚇 *Saint-Mandel-Tourelle* • *Wednesday 9 am-6 pm*

VIADUCT DES ARTISANS *See page 164*
Avenue Ledru-Rollin to rue de Charenton, 12th arr.
🚇 *Gare de Lyon • Tuesday-Sunday 10 am-6 pm;*
some shops close from noon to 2 pm or later

COVERED FOOD MARKETS

✦

BEAUVAU *See page 180*
Place d'Aligre, 12th arr. • 🚇 *Ledru-Rollin*
Tuesday-Sunday 7:30 am-12:30 pm

RIQUET
Corner of rue Riquet and rue Archereau, 12th arr. • 🚇 *Riquet*
Tuesday-Saturday 8:30 am-1 pm, 4-7:30 pm; Sunday 8:30 am-1 pm

The far northeast corner of Paris, comprising faded apartment blocks and colorless commercial buildings, is not a tourist destination. In the center of the market building, the Pause-Café offers something hot or alcoholic to drink. A corner store sells natural products. There is a wine shop and a place where household appliances can be repaired.

✦

BASTILLE *(formerly Richard Lenoir)* See page 170
Boulevard Richard Lenoir from rue Amelot to rue Saint-Sabin, 11th arr.
🚇 *Bastille • Thursday 7 am-2:30 pm; Sunday 7 am-3 pm*

BELLEVILLE
*Boulevard Belleville from rue Jean Pierre Timbaud/rue de
Menilmontant to rue du Faubourg du Temple/rue de Belleville, 11th arr.*
🚇 *Ménilmontant, Couronnes, Belleville*
Tuesday, Friday 7 am-2:30 pm

A wave of sound rolls over you, picks you up, and, if you're lucky, deposits
you in an eddy where you can catch your breath and get your bearings.
Brilliantly clothed African women, bearded orthodox Jews in black hats
and coats, small, determined Chinese women pushing their shopping
carts like battering rams, North African men with dark, lined faces and
round, brimless caps, all vie for the vendors' attention. There's no time
for merchants to stack their vegetables in pristine pyramids. Apples and
oranges are sold two or three kilos at a crack, potatoes and onions by the
sack, lettuce by the armload.

CHARONNE
*Boulevard de Charonne from rue de Charonne
to rue Alexandre Dumas, 11th arr. •* 🚇 *Alexandre Dumas*
Wednesday 7 am-2:30 pm; Saturday 7 am-3 pm

You can buy fish fresh from Normandy at Chez Laurent. Michel Chamillard has choucroute, duckling stuffed with prunes, and a sizzling rotisserie with a variety of poultry, rabbit, and turkey legs on his spits. Tiny white potatoes are heaped in the hot fat underneath. The hawking of fresh fruit goes like this: "*Fraises, mesdames, très, très belles et très solide!*" Grandjean's staff in red shirts and white aprons have ready-to-eat dishes, including the popular *brandade de morue*, sauté of pork with Indian spices, veal tongue with mushrooms, and beef with carrots.

PÈRE LACHAISE
Boulevard de Ménilmonant from rue des Panoyaux to rue Cendriers, 11th arr. • 🚇 *Ménilmontant*
Tuesday, Friday 7 am-2:30 pm

This small market offers quality produce and friendly vendors. When we visited, eggs were sold by weight in one-cent increments from the smallest to the largest.

POPINCOURT
Boulevard Richard Lenoir from rue Jean-Pierre Timbaud to rue Oberkampf, 11th arr.
🚇 *Oberkampf* • *Tuesday, Friday 7 am-2:30 pm*

The vendor of a staggering display of buttons, patches, threads, toggles, and other products, tools, and curiosities related to sewing, reviewed for us the decline of his business due to changes in style and the availability of ready-made clothing. Fishmongers do well here; four of them all had long queues of clients. One stand offers a large selection of dried fruit, including sugar-cured kumquats.

BERCY BARON-LE-ROY

Place Lachambeaudie and rue Baron le Roy, 12th arr.

🚇 *Dugommier* • *Wednesday 3-8 pm; Sunday, 7 am-3 pm*

Opened in February 2001, this market serves a part of Paris that is beginning to develop as a residential area relatively close to the city center. It's
small, but there is at least one of every kind of vendor. Bercy once lay
outside the city and was used by shippers who stored wine here to avoid
city taxes.

COURS DE VINCENNES

From boulevard de Picpus to avenue Dr. Arnold Netter, 12th arr.

🚇 *Porte de Vincennes, Nation*

Wednesday 7 am-2:30 pm; Saturday, 7 am-3 pm

In this market, there is little discussion of price, but many exchanges
on the weather, the elections, and the new asparagus. The herbalist has
preparations for slimming, for indigestion, and for stress, and the Tiger
Balm seller has charts of spines to show exactly where his product will
ease your pain. The offal vendor packs four kinds of tongue, as well as
sheep and veal brains in plastic containers, and displays chunks of clean
white intestine. The baker has an Acajou loaf made of rye flour with
almonds, walnuts, and raisins. His pound cake, called Quatre Quarts, has
a kilo each of flour, butter, sugar, and eggs.

DAUMESNIL

Boulevard Reuilly from place Felix Eboué to rue de Charenton, 12th arr.

🚇 *Daumesnil, Dugommier • Tuesday, Friday 7 am-2:30 pm*

This immense and busy market serves a neighborhood of apartment buildings. A double row of sycamores on both sides of the street shades the entire market. In May, the trees are heavy with spiky fruit that litters the sidewalks, distressing the cleaning crews. The buildings along the boulevard house small shops and services, providing aid and comfort beyond what can be found in the market. Most shoppers are older men and women who share friendly greetings and good-natured gossip.

LEDRU-ROLLIN

Avenue Ledru-Rollin from rue de Lyon to rue de Bercy, 12th arr.

🚇 *Gare de Lyon • Thursday 7 am-2:30 pm; Saturday 7 am-3 pm*

A sycamore-lined thoroughfare just a few blocks from Gare de Lyon is home to an unpretentious market. Half a dozen restaurants in the area prosper from the provisions available to them—Le Frégate for seafood, Le Quincy for specialties of the Auvergne, À la Biche au Bois for reliable game dishes. The Viaduc des Artisans is only a block away.

PONIATOWSKI

Boulevard Poniatowski from avenue Daumesnil to rue Picpus, 12th arr.

🚇 *Porte Dorée • Thursday 7 am-2:30 pm; Sunday 7 am-3 pm*

This neighborhood market would be even more remote had not the government originally located the Museum of the Arts of Africa and Oceania nearby (then moved it in 2006 to the recently completed Musée du Quai

Branly). A McDonald's on the corner is a bit disconcerting. There are not many stands here, or much to distinguish them from similar vendors elsewhere.

SAINT-ÉLOI

Rue de Reuilly at rue du Col and rue Rozanoff, 12th arr.

🚇 *Montgallet • Thursday 7 am-2:30 pm; Sunday 7 am-3 pm*

The arcade covering this market is worth something in bad weather. Vegetable, fish, and meat vendors look a bit fatigued, perhaps from the effort of competition with the Casino Supermarket across the street.

BELGRAND

Rue Belgrand from place Edith Piaf to rue Avenue Gambetta, 20th arr.

🚇 *Porte de Bagnolet, Gambetta*

Wednesday 7 am-2:30 pm; Saturday 7 am-3 pm

The Belgrand market seems to go on forever, offering a vast wealth of foodstuffs and clothing. It is remarkably diverse for a market so far from the center of Paris.

DAVOUT

Boulevard Davout from avenue de la Porte de Montreuil to place Marie de Mirabel, 20th arr.

🚇 *Porte de Montreuil • Tuesday, Friday 7 am-2:30 pm*

There are many produce stands in this market, and some novelties such as an herbalist who sells soap from Provence, and a cheese merchant from the island of Mauritius. The color and aroma of the hams at Jambon à l'Ancienne appeal to us, as does the poissonière Mechet, whose stand has a properly briny smell. He sells chunks of fish for soup at bargain prices.

MORTIER

Boulevard Mortier from avenue de la Porte de Ménilmontant
to rue Maurice Bertaux, 20th arr.
🚇 *Saint-Fargeau, Porte de Bagnolet*
Wednesday 7 am-2:30 pm; Sunday 7 am-3 pm

A gently sloping street with old sycamores lining broad sidewalks gives this market an appearance strangely akin to a London suburb. It has the neighborly feel particular to many outlying areas of Paris. Monsieur Petit offers pristine cheeses made at home from the milk of goats raised by him.

PYRÉNÉES

Rue des Pyrénées from rue de l'Ermitage
to rue de Ménilmontant, 20th arr. • 🚇 *Pyrénées, Jourdain*
Wednesday 7 am-2:30 pm; Sunday 7 am-3 pm

Display gets scant attention in this market. The ambiance is friendly, the presentation direct. We were drawn to Senteurs de Provence at 282, rue des Pyrénées, selling lavender, honey, candles, fabric, *santons*, and other regional products.

RÉUNION

Place de la Réunion, 20th arr. • 🚇 *Alexandre Dumas*
Thursday 7 am-2:30 pm; Sunday 7 am-3 pm

One of the larger markets on the outskirts of Paris, place de la Réunion caters to younger shoppers who have less to spend but bring the same insistence on *qualité-prix*, or value for money. At Grandjean, stainless steel pans are filled with cooked dishes ready to go: *tripes à la mode de Caen, legumes provençales, choucroute, sauté de porc à la Pékinoise*, freshly grilled sausages, and hot braised hams.

TÉLÉGRAPHE

Rue Télégraphe from rue de Belleville to the entrance
to the Cimetière de Belleville, 20th arr.
🚇 *Télégraphe* • *Wednesday 7 am-2:30 pm; Saturday 7 am-3 pm*

Water towers and a radio mast on the hilltop beside the cemetery signal this small neighborhood market in a distant part of Paris. There is the usual array of produce stands, cheese sellers, and fishmongers. Yannick Lebert's refrigerated butcher stand may give shoppers extra confidence.

MARKET STREET

✦

RUE D'ALIGRE *See page 176*
Rue d'Aligre, 12th arr. • 🚇 *Ledru-Rollin*
Tuesday-Saturday 8 am-5 pm; Sunday 8 am-1:30 pm

PARIS SOUTH

13th, 14th, and 15th arrondissements
Montparnasse, Porte de Vanves

MARKETPLACES

Marché Parisien de la Création · 194
Arts and Crafts Market

Marché du Livre Ancien et d'Occasion · 198
Antiquarian and Used Book Market

Marché aux Puces de Porte de Vanves · 202
Porte de Vanves Flea Market

Boutiques Stock · 206
Designer Clothing Shops

FOOD MARKETS

Marché Edgar Quinet · 207
Open-Air Market

Marché de Rungis · 210
Rungis Wholesale Food Market

✦

Neighborhood Markets · 213

Paris South Markets · 214

Marché Parisien de la Création

ARTS AND CRAFTS MARKET

BOULEVARD EDGAR QUINET FROM RUE HUYGHENS
TO RUE DU DÉPART, 14TH ARR.

🚋 EDGAR QUINET

SUNDAY 10 AM-7 PM

ALSO BOULEVARD RICHARD LENOIR, 11TH ARR.

🚋 BASTILLE

SATURDAY 9 AM-6 PM

THIS OUTDOOR ARTS AND CRAFTS MARKET STARTED IN THE 1990S IN THE PRETTY PARK WHERE THE MOUTON-Duvernet open-air food market is located. In 1997 the artists moved to a more accessible location, where the Edgar Quinet food market takes place twice a week. On Sunday, painters, sculptors, and craftspeople bring their work here and arrange it for viewing in small booths.

The art must be original and signed. If it is in series, there must be no more than ten copies. Oil and watercolor paintings intrigued us, but there are also ceramics, handmade clothing, fantasy hats, and sculpture in several media. Prices can range from a few dollars for a postcard-sized watercolor to a few hundred for a large oil painting.

This is a friendly market of more than a hundred artists, all looking for recognition. They are happy to talk about their work or anything else you may bring up. If the quality of the art is not up to gallery standards, much of it shows promise and all of it shows ambition. One young

woman was selling amusing miniature watercolors on postcards, reduced from her full-scale paintings.

We were delighted by small oil paintings, no larger than a guide-book, of the ubiquitous outdoor chairs in the Jardin du Luxembourg. Each arrangement seemed endowed with unique voices, and all were engaged in dialogues worth listening to. We bought one the first time we visited the market, for about a hundred dollars. A few years later they were still available, but the price had gone up.

We had a lengthy conversation with an artist who was using postage stamps as the basis for larger works. A small scene on a commemorative Vermeer stamp, for example, had been extended outward in all directions into a representation of the Dutch countryside. We were so intrigued we later wished we had bought one. But we'll be back another day.

A similar arts and crafts market takes place every Saturday, from 9 am to 6 pm, in the median plaza of boulevard Richard Lenoir (11th arrondissement), where the Bastille open-air food market is located on Thursday and Sunday.

Marché du Livre Ancien et d'Occasion

ANTIQUARIAN AND USED BOOK MARKET

PARC GEORGES BRASSENS, RUE BRANCION, 15TH ARR.

🚇 PORTE DE VANVES

SATURDAY-SUNDAY 9 AM-6 PM

THIS MARKET IS LOCATED IN TWO OPEN-AIR PAVILIONS SURROUNDED BY A HANDSOME IRON FENCE. A TILE ROOF floats on brick pillars over tables laden with books of every description— old, valuable, rare, or unique. As with other structures inspired by nineteenth-century tastes, the light, open feeling of this space might have been created by a spider working in wood and steel. Lighted globes hang in the arches overhead, but on cold, gloomy days neon tubes give the space a uniform brightness.

The market is divided into two parts linked by an open court. Standing alone on the brick pavers is a larger-than-life bronze sculpture of a butcher with half a carcass across his shoulders (signed A. Bucillo, 1991). He gives testimony to the slaughterhouse that occupied this space half a century ago.

Between seventy and one hundred vendors come here every weekend of the year, depending on the season and the weather. Goods range from magazines and books of photography to scholarly tomes, hardcover and softcover, some current and some long out of date. Many are spread out side-by-side on trestle tables so their titles and contents can easily be seen. Others are presented in boxes, or piled neatly (or stacked care-

lessly) according to the whim and style of the seller. Studious, well-dressed clients browse or search for particular items, chat quietly with the vendors, and encourage a love of books in the well-behaved children they've brought with them.

We were drawn to the *bandes-dessinées*, comic books between hard covers, like the adventures of Tintin, Asterix, Lucky Luke, and others. But the business of this market is mainly biography, history, novels, poems, and plays. When all is said and done, it is one of the calmest and most serious of all the markets of Paris.

It's worth stepping into the adjacent Georges Brassens Park, on the site that was once the Vaugirard slaughterhouse. Horses were auctioned here right into the mid-twentieth century. Now, walking paths wind through gently sculptured topography furnished with ponds, play structures, and outdoor sculptures. Among other interesting features are a scent garden for the blind, a beekeeping school, and a small vineyard.

Marché aux Puces de Porte de Vanves

AVENUE MARC SANGNIER AND AVENUE GEORGES LAFENESTRE, 14TH ARR.

🚋 PORTE DE VANVES

SATURDAY-SUNDAY 7 AM-7:30 PM

FROM THE VANVES MÉTRO STATION, WALK SOUTH INTO THE PLACE DE LA PORTE DE VANVES, THEN TURN LEFT INTO avenue Marc Sangnier. Vanves seems to us what Clignancourt was in the old days: a vast market where the variety is as great as the price range, and where with a bit of luck you can still find good buys.

The market makes an angle at the corner of avenues Sangnier and Lafenestre, with stands on both sides of the narrow sidewalk under big umbrellas or makeshift covers if the weather is unfriendly. Acacia trees give protection from the sun. There is no way easily to summarize the kind or number of things for sale here. Most of it is *brocante* (bric-a-brac), but according to an informant, dealers from Clignancourt still shop Vanves early in the morning for overlooked bargains.

Much of what we see appears to be from the twentieth century: glassware, table settings, ashtrays, furniture, and a large assortment of *bandes-dessinées*. What might we take home with us? Vintage glassware, asparagus and oyster platters, old linens, silverplated tableware, art deco vases, corkscrews made from dried grapevines—the list is virtually endless, depending on the instinct or obsession of the visitor.

We've looked for crystal Champagne flutes in every flea market and antique shop we've visited, and Vanves does not disappoint. We have enough now to give each of our four children a dozen. But there's much more: art nouveau objects such as coffee-table sculptures and Champagne buckets, furniture that was popular between the world wars, and classical pieces such as armoires, bedside tables, and *tables de ferme* (farmhouse tables). With luck, we might someday find an old *garde-manger*, a wooden cage that hung in a cool place near the kitchen to keep leftovers, cheeses, and vegetables.

A visit to a flea market is bit like peering in the window of an elderly neighbor couple's apartment. They've kept everything from their marriages and their visits to foreign countries, and now they are ready to sell out and move into a retirement home. At the market, collecting passions are displayed like the habits of a lifetime, whether ceramic jugs or African wood carvings. The family traditions are displayed there too: linen napkins with embroidered initials of grandparents, and table settings handed down from one or more of their families. One can't help feeling a bit embarrassed, yet one can't help looking.

You can spend half an hour in the Vanves flea market, or half a day with a lunch break at the Café Didot, at the intersection of the avenues Sangnier and Lafenestre. Or you can walk up to the boulevard Brune on Sunday and gather the makings of a picnic in the food market there. If a ham sandwich is enough to soothe the savage beast, food stands located throughout the market will provide it. There may be a soccer game under way on the adjacent field. There's a lot to see, a lot to think about, and perhaps even a purchase to make before leaving.

Boutiques Stock

THE FRENCH WORD FOR A LOW-PRICE OUTLET IS *STOCK*. THE WORD IS FOUND ON SHOP-FRONTS IN THIS PART OF Paris, in various combinations with the store name or specialty. Clothing has been *dégriffé*, meaning that the original label has been removed and the goods offered at reduced prices. Men and women of all ages prowl for bargains, but the dominant animals in this jungle are young people seeking big names at small cost. When their working day ends they crowd the sidewalks, and in the busiest shops you hear little more than hangers scraping on steel rods and cries of delight as hot designer outfits are recognized and claimed.

Some shops are specialized by designer (one shop carries only Cacherel), by item (shirts and blouses), or age (6-16), but the majority has standard items of clothing, mainly for women. There's a holiday feeling, perhaps because of the bright lights and enthusiasm. We loved the casual bonhomie of this street, especially the organ grinder who was working his machine on the sidewalk when we passed by. Neighborhood children clustered around without the slightest thought of commerce in their heads, simply enjoying themselves listening to the music.

Marché Edgar Quinet

OPEN-AIR MARKET

BOULEVARD EDGAR QUINET FROM BOULEVARD RASPAIL TO
RUE DU DÉPART, 14TH ARR.

🚇 EDGAR QUINET, VAVIN

WEDNESDAY 7 AM- 2:30 PM; SATURDAY 7 AM- 3 PM

ONE OF THE FINEST FEATURES OF THIS PART OF PARIS IS THE CALM, WOODED EXPANSE OF THE MONTPARNASSE cemetery along boulevard Edgar Quinet. The market is spread out next to it, a broad aisle with stalls on both sides in the tree-lined median plaza. At the west end of the market the Montparnasse tower rises like a giant tombstone. If there remains any doubt in a traveler's mind whether permitting a modern high-rise building in this part of Paris was a good idea, a visit to the Edgar Quinet market will resolve it.

Spring and autumn are obviously different in the markets, and this one illustrates the point. In autumn we found several presentations of the ever-popular snails packed with garlic and butter (*escargots Provençale, escargots Bourguignonne*). A

dozen varieties of fresh and stunningly beautiful mushrooms were laid out with pine boughs separating them; waxy *girolles*, gray *pleurottes*, orange *chanterelles*, fat brown *cèpes*, and chalky white *champignons de Paris*; also the meaty shiitake, the oddly cleft *pied de mouton*, and somber black *trompettes de la mort*, bizarre but delicious.

There are many examples of seasonal *charcuterie* made from ham and game, and there is an ever-present aroma of *choucroute* steaming in kettles. Two big rotisseries serve a brisk takeout business. On one, pork ribs glistening with sauce are stripped off the spits onto a butcher block, cut up, and speedily wrapped in aluminum foil for waiting patrons. We rarely escape without adding a few ribs to our market basket.

Spring offers some different choices. Vegetables are prominent, and the aroma of fresh strawberries reaches out to us from a distance. The florist at the east end of the market takes credit cards; his selection is ample and his prices are right. Eric Cazar specializes in goat cheeses, and sells the wines that best accompany them. He proposed a red Chinon that we've tried and liked. J. L. Testard sells fresh morels; who cares if they come from Turkey, they're fabulous!

Farther along, you can take home as many bras in different colors as you may want for €2 each. We note a large array of sunglasses in hard cases, and across the way, a huge selection of DVDs, including some of our favorite Tintin stories. It seems to us a sure-fire method of teaching French to our grandchildren. M. Chereau sells four different tools for trimming fingernails and toenails, a specialization new to us. Beggars at each end often enclose this market like sad parentheses, but if you leave a few cents with them you'll experience a touch of grace.

Marché de Rungis

RUNGIS WHOLESALE FOOD MARKET

IN RUNGIS, SOUTH OF PARIS NEAR ORLY AIRPORT

NO MÉTRO SERVICE

TUESDAY-SUNDAY 2-8 AM

for information, see www.visitrungis.com

THIS DISTRIBUTION CENTER WAS ESTABLISHED IN 1969 WHEN LES HALLES, THE FOOD MARKET IN THE CENTER OF Paris for more than a century, was relocated south of the city. You have to make special arrangements to visit, and when you get there you can't buy anything. But if food in any and all of its forms interests you, as it does us, you'll want to see first hand how Paris and the surrounding region arranges to feed itself at such a high level of quality, day in and day out. We were picked up at our hotel at 4 am and got to Rungis about 5. Everything is vast: 575 acres, 45,000 square feet under roof, and 20,000 buyers every day. The markets open in the order of a French meal: the fish market at 2 am, meat at 3, vegetables and cheese at 4, and flowers last of all. The fish and seafood hall is somewhat reminiscent of Tokyo's incredible Tsukiji market. There were some big tuna, as well as crayfish, shrimp, and lobster (*les crustacées*) at one end of the hall, and shellfish (*les coquillages*) at the other. It was late when we arrived, and men were already hosing down the floors, dumping ice, and kicking through a mess of broken Styrofoam boxes.

We went into the meat hall, a forest of hanging carcasses of beef, lamb, and veal, and then on to the offal hall. Pork is done in a separate building: We were somewhat prepared by our visits to the markets, but it was still a shock to see rows of pig's heads, piles of trotters, and long lines of snouts and tails. Skins from the heads were hung up like limp Halloween masks.

The birds in the poultry building still have their heads on (and many their feet as well). Buyers believe this helps them judge quality and freshness, and that they keep longer that way. Then came the cheese hall, a sumptuously aromatic place with pile after pile of familiar cheeses in boxes. A worker was slicing Emmenthal into chunks using a wire with small wood handles such as a potter uses to take work off the wheel.

We continued to the fruit and vegetable halls, four long buildings packed with produce, and arrayed so that we could see from one end to the other, the length of an airport runway. The distances are so great that workers get around on bicycles. Last was the flower hall, where the flowers were so fresh they didn't need to be in water. Rosebuds were curled as tight as snail shells, and the peonies were balled like babies' fists. After so many noisy, cold halls, this one was quiet and relatively warm.

Few chefs come to Rungis to shop. Nowadays they rely on specialized middlemen who shop for them and deliver to their restaurants. Fax and the *minitel* (now internet) have made a big difference in the way the market functions, since tradespeople don't have to stay up half the night on the telephone to place orders.

The market continues to evolve in other ways. For example, there are more prepared foods like cooked shrimp and skewered meat ready to barbecue. And improvements in distribution work in favor of small-scale merchants who buy in limited quantities. It isn't like Les Halles, with its medieval atmosphere, wooden carts full of produce, and early morning onion soup. We feel lucky to have experienced the old market before it was taken down and moved, but we were impressed by the size and efficiency of the one that has taken its place.

NEIGHBORHOOD MARKETS

Several neighborhoods have clusters of shops on the same or adjacent streets that feature the same or similar kinds of goods. Knowing about such neighborhoods is useful if you're looking for a particular item: you can compare quality, cost, and condition without going all over the city.

Shops with low-priced women's clothing and goods by the yard begin in place du Caire, continue in passage du Caire, and end at boulevard Étienne Marcel in the 2nd arrondissement (Métros: Sentier, Bonne Nouvelle, and Strasbourg Saint-Denis). Music and musical instruments can be found in the 8th arrondissement in rue de Rome and rue de Madrid, near the Gare Saint-Lazare (Métro: Saint-Lazare). Leather and furs are sold on rue d'Hauteville in the 10th arrondissement (Métro: Poissonnière). Also in the 10th, two blocks of the rue de Paradis contain a dozen shops selling stemware, glass, crystal, and china (Métro: Gare de l'Est). Everything and anything related to fabrics is available in one of the shops in rue d'Orsel, near the fabric store Saint-Pierre (Métro: Barbès-Rochechouart).

Rue du Faubourg Saint-Antoine, from east of the Bastille opera house to the Saint-Antoine hospital in the 12th arrondissement, is a warren of furniture stores (Métro: Ledru Rollin). The little passage du Chantier is especially intriguing; with its huge, square cobblestones it looks like a world that existed before the French Revolution. Don't expect a romantic Parisian scene here. Rue Saint-Antoine is cacophonous with auto horns and reeks of exhaust, as commerce proceeds at a furious pace.

Paris South Markets

13th, 14th, and 15th arrondissements

ART, ANTIQUE, AND FLEA MARKETS

✦

MARCHÉ DU LIVRE ANCIEN ET D'OCCASION *See page 198*

Parc Georges Brassens, rue Brancion, 15th arr.

🚇 *Porte de Vanves • Saturday-Sunday 9 am-6 pm*

MARCHÉ PARISIEN DE LA CRÉATION *See page 194*

Boulevard Edgar Quinet from rue Huyghens to rue du Départ, 14th arr.

🚇 *Edgar Quinet • Sunday 10 am-7 pm*

MARCHÉ AUX PUCES DE PORTE DE VANVES *See page 202*

Avenue Marc Sangnier and avenue Georges Lafenestre, 14th arr.

🚇 *Porte de Vanves • Saturday-Sunday 7 am-7:30 pm*

OPEN-AIR FOOD MARKETS

✦

AUGUSTE BLANQUI

Boulevard Auguste Blanqui from place d'Italie to rue Barrault, 13th arr.

🚇 *place d'Italie • Friday 7 am-2:30 pm, Sunday 7 am-3 pm*

This market begins in place d'Italie, with its movie theater and modern buildings, and continues into the tree-lined boulevard Auguste Blanqui. There are more shoppers of all nationalities than in markets farther from the center of Paris, creating a true multiethnic meeting place.

BOBILLOT

Rue Bobillot from place de Rungis to rue de la Colonie, 13th arr.

🚊 *Maison Blanche* • *Tuesday, Friday 7 am-2:30 pm*

Old sycamore trees shade this relaxed and friendly market. Near the place de Rungis there is a pretty park. High school students come and go through a gate in the middle of the market, enlivening the site.

JEANNE D'ARC

At the church Notre Dame de la Gare, Place Jeanne d'Arc, 13th arr.

🚊 *Nationale* • *Thursday 7 am-2:30 pm, Sunday 7 am-3 pm*

The church of Notre Dame de la Gare in the middle of a broad plaza is the focal point of this market. What a surprise to find silver fox and mink coats on sale at one of the stands. The fish at Visery are fresh to our eyes, and our noses concur. Jean-Luc Felten, the *charcutière*, has a smile and a quip for every patron, and a line of tasty little tarts:; spinach, brioche with sausage and pistachio, a *millefeuilles* of ham and cheese, and a *bouchée à la reine* ready to pop in the oven.

MAISON BLANCHE

Avenue d'Italie from rue du Tage to allée Marc Chagall, 13th arr.

🚊 *Maison Blanche* • *Thursday 7 am-2:30 pm, Sunday 7 am-3 pm*

Small, low-key, friendly, this market offers a balanced selection of food, clothing, and services. La Corbeille Normandie sells *confetti* (confit) of giblets and a *rillette* of duck. A rotisserie offers farm-raised chickens, whole or half, small, medium, or large, and priced to go.

SALPÉTRIÈRE

At the entrance to the Pitié-Salpétrière hospital,
boulevard de l'Hôpital, 13th arr.

🚇 *Saint-Marcel • Tuesday, Friday 7 am-2:30 pm*

The Métro rumbles overhead, and after a rainstorm the platform leaks on the market below. But the architectural grandeur of the adjacent Hôpital la Pitié-Salpétrière makes it worthwhile. There are vegetable stands, a fishmonger, a butcher, a *charcuterie*, and some practical clothing.

VINCENT AURIOL

From rue Jeanne d'Arc to rue du Chevaleret, 13th arr.

🚇 *Nationale, Chevaleret • Wednesday 7 am-2:30 pm, Saturday 7 am-3 pm*

The columns and girders of the Métro, which passes overhead with an intermittent rumble, and a row of young oak trees planted on each side frame the market. Road traffic is noisy, but the merchants are friendly and welcoming, and all the usual market stands are represented.

ALÉSIA

Rue de la Glacière from rue de la Santé and rue d'Alésia, 14th arr.

🚇 *Glacière • Wednesday 7 am-2:30 pm, Saturday 7 am-3 pm*

Tall, lacy acacia trees maintain a comfortable temperature and create pleasant ambient light. The market offers the usual fare and is easy to stroll and study as it spreads out against a fence along the sidewalk. The cheese shop has wheels of Comté and Emmenthal big enough to feed the quartier.

BRANCUSI
Place Constantin Brancusi, 14th arr.

🚇 *Gaîté (if open), Edgar Quinet • Saturday 9 am-2 pm*

This tiny market is advertised as *biologique* (organic), and some stands make it honest. The setting, in a severe little square amid the vast agglomeration of apartment buildings south of Montparnasse, is not interesting, but the vendors are pleasant and accommodating.

BRUNE
Boulevard Brune from rue Didot to rue Raymond Losserand, 14th arr.

🚇 *Porte de Vanves • Thursday 7 am-2:30 pm, Sunday 7 am-3 pm*

Clothing, household goods, and a long run of vegetable and fruit stands interspersed with fishmongers, butchers, bakers, and cheese sellers make this a well-stocked market. Sausages of Jacquet de Nanterres are impressive, as well as canned quail with duck liver, confit of duck, and other Dordogne products. The butcher Goulet boned two rabbit haunches with the speed and precision of a cardiac surgeon. Robert Foucat has a variety of spices in small cellophane bags, ideal to take home as gifts.

EDGAR QUINET *See page 207*
Boulevard Edgar Quinet from boulevard Raspail
to rue du Départ, 14th arr. • 🚇 *Edgar Quinet, Raspail*
Wednesday 7 am-2:30 pm, Saturday 7 am-3 pm

MOUTON-DUVERNET *(Montrouge)*

In the square bounded by rue Brezin, rue Saillard, rue Boulard,
and rue Mouton-Duvernet, 14th arr.

🚇 *Mouton-Duvernet* • *Tuesday, Friday 7 am-2:30 pm*

One of the loveliest sites in Paris, this one shows us again that markets in squares have more charm than markets on sidewalks. Young elms provide shade, three aisles of stands are comfortably close, and extra tarps stretched overhead keep off sun and rain. Lebanese specialties are prepared on the spot. The cheeses of Jean-Jacques Lainé have a country character, with bits of straw and ash still clinging to their rinds.

VILLEMAIN

Place Lieutenant S. Piobetta from rue d'Alésia
to avenue Villemain, 14th arr.

🚇 *Plaisance* • *Wednesday 7 am-2:30 pm, Sunday 7 am-3 pm*

A typically friendly but unremarkable neighborhood market, this one comprises about twenty stands, easily accessible because of their location on two sides of a triangular garden. The produce is fresh and appealing. Michel and Christine Pérus sell pristine cheeses and yogurts.

CERVANTES

Place Wassily Kandinsky, opposite nos. 49-51, rue Bargue, 15th arr.

🚇 *Volontaires* • *Wednesday 7 am-2:30 pm, Saturday 7 am-3 pm*

High-rise apartment buildings tower over this market. The location is somewhat colorless, but the market has personality, perhaps because of the friendliness of vendors unaccustomed to visitors from a distant part of Paris. Half the market is under an arcade, important if the day is damp.

CONVENTION
Rue de la Convention from rue de Vaugirard
to place Charles Vallin, 15th arr.

🚇 *Convention* • *Tuesday, Thursday 7 am-2:30 pm, Sunday 7 am-3 pm*

Dickensian in its vastness and complexity, this market along both sides of rue de la Convention is one of the most difficult to negotiate on market days. Nevertheless, it is rich in sounds and sights, with a mixture of buyers and sellers of many nationalities. It's a mystery how such an immense quantity of meat, fish, poultry, and produce can move from vendors' tables to shoppers' baskets, all in a setting of good-humored haggling. Snails in the shell and frogs legs *en brochette* are ready for the grill.

GRENELLE
Boulevard de Grenelle from rue de Lourmel
to rue du Commerce, 15th arr.

🚇 *Dupleix, La Motte Picquet-Grenelle*
Wednesday 7 am-2:30 pm, Sunday 7 am-3 pm

A special popularity invests the Sunday markets, and Grenelle is no exception. La Ferme du Poirier Rond, from Saint-Vrain, draws us to compare goat cheeses. Another nice cheese stall is La Ferme de l'Isle. Nearby is a choice fishmonger, Robert Bourgeois, and a bit farther on is D. Loeb with farm-fresh produce. J. C. Desormeau charmingly characterizes his oysters as the foie gras of the sea.

✦

RUE DAGUERRE

From rue Boulard to avenue du Général Leclerc, 14th arr.

🚇 *Denfert Rochereau.*

Tuesday-Saturday 10 am-7 pm; Sunday morning

Rue Daguerre is very much a neighborhood affair, with ample offerings of fruit, vegetables, meat, and fish. At Daguerre Marée, shrimp and langoustines form great glistening pyramids, sweet to smell and good to the pocketbook. There's a fine chocolatier and an excellent cheese shop. Try the tiny restaurant, Le Moule à Gâteau, at the corner of rue Boulard.

OTHER MARKETS

✦

BOUTIQUES STOCK *See page 206*

Rue d'Alésia from rue Didot to place Victor Basch, 13th arr.

🚇 *Plaisance, Alésia* • *Tuesday-Sunday 10 am-6 pm*

(as of June 2006 the Alésia metro station was closed for renovation)

HALLE AUX POISSONS

Rue Castagnary at rue Morillon, 15th arr.

🚇 *Plaisance* • *Tuesday-Saturday, 9 am-1 pm*

This odd little market is tucked under the rail line south of the Montparnasse station. If you approach from the south, you're alerted to its existence by a nearly full-size fishing boat painted blue, white, and red (the colors of the French flag) perched on the berm, a sailor standing in the bow. Neon letters on the side of the vessel spell out "*Gloire a nos marins pecheurs*" (Glory to our fishermen). The market is small and friendly, with Disney-like scenes of castles and landscapes on the walls.

MARCHÉ DE RUNGIS *See page 210*
In Rungis, near Orly Airport • No Métro service
Tuesday-Sunday 2 am-8 am
For information, see www.visitrungis.com

Suggested Daily Itineraries

HOW TO ORGANIZE YOUR PRECIOUS TIME IN PARIS IS, OF COURSE, AN INDIVIDUAL DECISION FOR EVERY TRAVELER. There will always be important tourist sites you intended to visit but couldn't find time for. A balanced and fully satisfying visit would include some of the great sites—Napoleon's tomb, the Musee d'Orsay, the Jardin de Luxembourg—along with some lesser-known places like the Saint-Pierre fabric market, a covered food market, and one of the antique villages. To help you incorporate some of these alternative experiences, we've suggested daily itineraries. They are ambitious, and you may choose to do only one, or a part of one that best fits your schedule. But they offer some ideas to get you started.

MONDAY

Paris North and Right Bank

✦

MARCHÉ AUX PUCES DE CLIGNANCOURT
Clignancourt Flea Market
CARROUSEL DU LOUVRE *Carrousel Shopping Center*
LOUVRE DES ANTIQUAIRES *Louvre of Antique Dealers*

This is the quietest day at Clignancourt, and most other markets are closed on Monday. After Clignancourt in the morning, stop for lunch at Carrousel du Louvre, then shop for antiques at the Louvre of Antique Dealers.

TUESDAY

Paris West and Right Bank

✦

POINT DU JOUR *Open-Air Food Market*

RUE DE L'ANNONCIATION

Market Street

VILLAGE SUISSE DES ANTIQUITÉS

Swiss Village Antiques

RUE CLER *Market Street*

Visit the Point du Jour market and rue de l'Annonciation in the morning, stop for lunch in Passy, and shop for antiques in the Swiss Village. If time permits, end the day at rue Cler.

WEDNESDAY

Paris East and North

✦

MARCHÉ AUX VIEUX PAPIERS

Old Papers Market

MARCHÉ BARBÈS

Open-Air Food Market

MARCHÉ SAINT-PIERRE

Saint-Pierre Fabric Market

MARCHÉ LA CHAPELLE *Covered Market*

Visit the Old Papers Market or the Marché Barbès, continue to the fabric market or La Chapelle, and have a late lunch in one of Montmartre's charming small restaurants.

THURSDAY
Left Bank, Paris West and Right Bank

✦

MARCHÉ RASPAIL
Open-Air Market
MARCHÉ AUX TIMBRES ET AUX CARTES TÉLÉPHONIQUES
Postage Stamp and Telephone Card Market
VILLAGE SAINT-PAUL
Saint-Paul Antique Village

Begin at boulevard Raspail, go on to the postage stamp and phone card market, have a light lunch on the Champs-Elysées, and end in the Village Saint-Paul.

FRIDAY
Left Bank and Paris South

✦

MARCHÉ MONGE
Open-Air Food Market
MARCHÉ AUX VIEUX PAPIERS
Old Papers Market
BOTIQUES STOCK
Designer Clothing

Begin at place Monge, continue to rue Mouffetard, where there are a number of small restaurants, then go on to rue d'Alésia stock shops.

SATURDAY A
Paris South

✦

PORTE DE VANVES MARCHÉ AUX PUCES
Porte de Vanves Flea Market

MARCHÉ EDGAR QUINET *Open-Air Food Market*

MARCHÉ DU LIVRE ANCIEN ET D'OCCASION
Antiquarian and Used Book Market

RUE DAGUERRE *Market Street*

Begin at Porte de Vanves, continue to rue Daguerre, and have lunch in the area. Alternatively, begin at the Edgar Quinet market, stop for lunch in Montparnasse, and continue to the Antiquarian and Used Book Market.

SATURDAY B
Right Bank and Paris West

✦

MARCHÉ SAXE-BRETEUIL
Open-Air Market

RUE PONCELET
Market Street

MARCHÉ AUX FLEURS ET AUX OISEAUX
Flower and Bird Markets

Begin at Saxe-Breteuil market, continue to rue Poncelet, have lunch in the Les Halles-Palais Royale area, and end at the Flower Market on Île de la Cité.

Right Bank and Paris East

✦

MARCHÉ AUX OISEAUX

Bird Market

MARCHÉ BASTILLE

Open-Air Market

RUE MONTORGEUIL

Market Street

Begin at Île de la Cité Bird Market, go on to the Bastille, and to rue Montorgeuil with a lunch stop there or near the Palais Royale area.

SUNDAY B

Paris East and Paris South

✦

RUE D'ALIGRE

Market Street

MARCHÉ BEAUVAU

Covered Market

MARCHÉ PARISIEN DE LA CRÉATION

Arts and Crafts Market

Begin at rue d'Aligre open market and adjacent Beauvau covered market, stop at the Baron Rouge for a glass of wine, continue to boulevard Edgar Quinet art market, stop for lunch near the Edgar Quinet metro station.

Restaurant Listings

FINDING A RESTAURANT IN PARIS IS EASY, BUT FINDING ONE THAT FITS THE MOOD OF THE MOMENT, WHERE HONEST food is served, where one is treated with courtesy and leaves with a sense of gratitude, is not. Not every restaurant in this list is guaranteed to satisfy these criteria. We've tried most of them ourselves, often for lunch; the names of a few came to us from trusted friends. If you're using a credit card, make sure it's accepted before you order. The English-language restaurant guide we like is Michael A. Bernstein, *The Paris Guide*, Fourth Edition. The *Zagat Survey* is also handy and useful. In French we use *Pudlo Paris: le point 2006*, and consult www.pagesrestos.com. However you find the restaurant of your dreams, *bonne chance, et bon appétit!*

1ST ARRONDISSEMENT

✦

AU PIED DE COCHON
6, rue Coquillière • ☎ *01 40 13 77 00* • *Daily, 24 hours* • 🚇 *les Halles*

This venerable establishment once drew its victuals from the huge Les Halles market. Famous for everything porcine, especially trotters, it has a buzz and savoir faire that make it worth a visit.

CHEZ PAULINE
5, rue Villedo • ☎ *01 42 96 20 70* • 🚇 *Palais Royal, Bourse*
Monday-Saturday to 10:30 pm; closed Saturday lunch and Sunday

Friends of ours were virtually adopted here, demonstrating how a traditional bistro can enrich your life beyond the food they serve.

LES CARTES POSTALES

7, rue Gomboust, • ☎ *01 42 61 02 93* • 🚇 *Pyramides*

Tuesday-Sunday to 10:30 pm; closed Saturday lunch, Sunday, and Monday dinner

A talented Japanese chef serves innovative dishes in a charming venue.

RESTAURANT DU PALAIS ROYAL

110, Galerie de Valois—Jardin du Palais Royal • ☎ *01 40 20 00 27*

Daily to 10:30 pm; closed Saturday (October-April) and Sunday (summer)

🚇 *Palais Royal-Musée du Louvre*

This is a wonderful location in the heart of the heart of Paris, with a traditional setting and comfort food.

RESTAURANT PAUL

15, place Dauphine/35, quai des Orfevres • ☎ *01 43 54 21 48*

Tuesday-Sunday to 10:30 pm; closed Monday • 🚇 *Cité*

You can dine outdoors on the Seine side or in the lovely (and quiet) place Dauphine. Inside are dark wood and banquettes, and classic dishes at reasonable prices. Service is friendly and impeccable.

WILLI'S WINE BAR

13, rue des Petits-Champs • ☎ *01 42 61 05 09*

Monday-Saturday to 11 pm; closed Sunday

🚇 *Bourse/Palais Royal-Musée du Louvre*

Willi's has gotten high marks over the years from all the reputable French and American reviewers, and deserves them.

2ND ARRONDISSEMENT

✦

CHEZ GEORGES

1, rue du Mail • ☎ *01 42 60 07 11* • 🚇 *Bourse, Sentier*
Monday-Saturday to 9:45 pm; closed Sunday

This is a classic bistro serving classic dishes near perfection.

L'ESCARGOT MONTORGUEIL

38, rue Montorgueil • ☎ *01 42 36 83 51* • 🚇 *les Halles*
Monday-Saturday to 11 pm; closed all day Sunday and Monday lunch

This lovely small bistro has descended from another age; standard fare, but perfect ambience.

3RD ARRONDISSEMENT

✦

AU BASCOU

38, rue Réamur • ☎ *01 42 72 69 25* • 🚇 *Arts et Métiers*
Monday-Friday to 10:30 pm; closed Saturday and Sunday

Come here for Basque cooking at its best in a friendly and informal environment.

4TH ARRONDISSEMENT

✦

LA BARACANE

38, rue des Tournelles • ☎ 01 42 71 43 33 • 🚇 Bastille
Monday-Friday to midnight; closed Saturday and Sunday

A great bistro featuring the cooking of the southwest; service a bit slow but atmosphere engaging.

BENÔIT

20, rue Saint-Martin • ☎ 01 42 72 25 76 • 🚇 Châtelet
Monday-Saturday to 10 pm; closed Saturday lunch and Sunday

A classic in all respects, from the decor to the menu; its one Michelin star is well deserved.

LE BISTRO DU DÔME

2, rue de la Bastille • ☎ 01 48 04 88 44 • Daily to 11 pm • 🚇 Bastille

You will find here the same good management and good seafood as one finds at Le Dôme and its neighboring bistro in the 14th arrondissement.

BOFINGER

5, rue de la Bastille • ☎ 01 42 72 87 82 • Daily to 1 am • 🚇 Bastille

The oldest brasserie in Paris (1864), with turn-of-the-century decor and a standard menu.

MA BOURGOGNE

19, place des Vosges • ☎ 01 42 78 44 64
Daily 8 am to 1:30 am • 🚇 Bastille

In a welcoming corner location, this is the place for a coffee and croissant, a salad, or a drink; limited food menu.

PETIT BOFINGER

6, rue de la Bastille • ☎ *01 42 72 05 23* • *Daily to 1 am* • 🚇 *Bastille*

A fabulous fallback when the main restaurant across the street is full.
Also located at:

• *20, boulevard Montmartre, 9th*

• *46, boulevard du Montparnasse, 14th*

• *10, place Maréchal Juin, 17th*

5TH ARRONDISSEMENT

✦

BRASSERIE BALZAR

49, rue des Écoles • ☎ *01 43 54 13 67*

Daily to midnight • 🚇 *Cluny-la Sorbonne*

This beloved brasserie almost disappeared a few years ago when new
owners took over. It survives with a revised menu, the same art deco interior, attentive service, and reliable dishes classically prepared.

CHANTAIRELLE

17, rue Laplace • ☎ *01 46 33 18 59* • 🚇 *Maubert-Mutualité*

Monday-Saturday to 10:30 pm; closed Saturday lunch and Sunday

You'll find superb country specialties of the Auvergne in this modern
bistro.

LA MAISON

1, rue de la Bûcherie • ☎ *01 43 29 73 57* • 🚇 *Maubert-Mutualité*

Tuesday-Sunday to 11 pm; closed all day Monday, Tuesday lunch

A lovely small place with bushels of charm and an excellent menu; don't be concerned if the bulldog, Polo, licks the last of the gravy from your dangling hand.

MOISSONIER

28, rue des Fossés-Saint-Bernard • ☎ *01 43 29 87 65*

Tuesday-Saturday to 10 pm; closed Sunday and Monday

🚇 *Cardinal Lemoine*

Food is in the Lyonnais bistro tradition—lots of it and quite good.

AU MOULIN À VENT

20, rue des Fossés-Saint-Bernard • ☎ *01 43 54 99 37*

Tuesday-Saturday to 11 pm; closed Saturday lunch,

all day Sunday and Monday • 🚇 *Cardinal Lemoine*

This traditional bistro has hardly changed since World War II, though meat specialties have kept pace with demand.

LE REMINET

3, rue des Grands-Degrés • ☎ *01 44 07 04 24*

Closed Tuesday-Wednesday • 🚇 *Maubert-Mutualité*

A long, narrow room is made romantic with candles, mirrors, and chandeliers. An appealing menu, but tables are too close for comfort.

LA RÔTISSERIE DU BEAUJOLAIS

19, quai de la Tournelle • ☎ *01 43 54 17 47* • 🚇 *Maubert-Mutualité*

Tuesday-Sunday to 10:15 pm; closed Monday

The same owner as the fabled Tour d'Argent across the way, this Lyonnais-style bistro is lively and stocks all ten crus of Beaujolais.

6TH ARRONDISSEMENT

✦

ALLARD

1, rue de l'Eperon (old entrance around the corner at
41, rue Saint-André-des-Arts) • ☎ *01 43 26 48 23*
Monday-Saturday to 11 pm; closed Sunday • 🚇 *Saint-Michel, Odéon*

We've been up and down about this place; it may depend on who is in the kitchen; sometimes it's incredibly good, and sometimes just okay.

LA BASTIDE ODÉON

7, rue Corneille • ☎ *01 43 26 03 65* • 🚇 *Odéon, Luxembourg*
Tuesday-Saturday to 10:30 pm; closed Sunday and Monday

Proud of their nouvelle menu and their Provençale tilt, they are good, but at a price.

LE BISTROT D'HENRI

16, rue Princesse • ☎ *01 46 33 51 12*
Daily until 11:30 pm • 🚇 *Mabillon*

Cigarette smoke drives us away, but the *qualité-prix* brings us back. Tables from recycled sewing machines, moleskin banquettes, and an open kitchen conspire to create hustle and charm.

LES BOOKINISTES

53, quai des Grands-Augustins • ☎ *01 43 25 45 94* • 🚇 *Saint-Michel*

Monday-Saturday to 11 pm; closed Saturday lunch and Sunday

Views of the Quai, and a sense of high energy; through several visits the food never disappointed us, though it's a bit pricey.

BOUILLON RACINE

3, rue Racine • ☎ *01 44 32 15 60*

Daily until midnight • 🚇 *Odéon, Cluny-la Sorbonne*

Perhaps the only Belgian restaurant in Paris, its selection of native beers accompanies classic dishes of France's northern neighbor; high-quality art deco interior, a quiet environment, and a very pleasant bar.

BRASSERIE LIPP

151, boulevard Saint-Germain • ☎ *01 45 48 53 91*

Daily noon to 1 am • 🚇 *Saint-Germain-des-Prés*

The food may be mundane and the service somewhat casual, but this is where France's intellectual and political classes act like ordinary mortals with appetites. Try to be seated on the ground floor.

BRASSERIE LUTÉTIA

Hotel Lutétia, 23, rue de Sèvres • ☎ *01 49 54 46 76*

Daily noon to midnight • 🚇 *Sèvres-Babylone*

This wonderful brasserie is on the sidewalk level of the glamorous art deco Hôtel Lutétia. Shellfish in season are expensive, but to die for.

LE CHERCHE-MIDI

22, rue du Cherche-Midi • ☎ 01 45 48 27 44

Daily until 11:45 pm • 🚇 Sèvres-Babylone

We were nearly buried by a busload of Japanese tourists, but we and they were served promptly and ate well enough; a good port in a storm.

L'EPI DUPIN

11, rue Dupin • ☎ 01 42 22 64 56 • 🚇 Sèvres-Babylone

Monday-Friday to 11 pm;

closed Saturday-Sunday, and Monday lunch

Interesting dishes at acceptable prices, but getting a reservation has been difficult.

FISH LA BOISSONNERIE

Restaurant Méditerranéan, 69, rue de Seine • ☎ 01 43 54 34 69

Closed Monday • 🚇 Mabillon

We got to know co-owner Juan Sanchez when he opened La Dernière Goute, a small wine shop around the corner. Naturally we became clients when he opened Fish. The fresh catch and the pasta always please us.

LA RÔTISSERIE D'EN FACE

2, rue Christine • ☎ 01 43 26 40 98 • 🚇 Odéon

Sunday-Thursday to 11 pm; Friday and Saturday to 11:30 pm

closed Saturday lunch and all day Sunday

The second kitchen of Jacques Cagna, whose main establishment is a few steps away, offers a hearty menu and pleasant service.

✦

LE BAMBOCHE

15, rue de Babylone • ☎ *01 45 49 14 40*

Daily to 10 pm; closed Sunday lunch • 🚇 *Sèvres-Babylone*

For their elegant portions, interesting choices, and romantic dining room, we keep going back.

AU BON ACCUEIL

14, rue de Monttessuy • ☎ *01 47 05 46 11* • 🚇 *Alma-Marceau*

Monday-Saturday to 10 pm; closed Saturday lunch and Sunday

A traditional bistro with modern elements, it's always busy, so book ahead.

LE MAUPERTU

94, boulevard de la Tour Maubourg • ☎ *01 45 51 37 96*

Daily to 10 pm; closed Sunday dinner • 🚇 *École Militaire*

This classic small restaurant has a local clientele, an appealing menu, and reasonable prices. A good wine list adds to its luster.

LES MINISTÈRES

30, rue du Bac • ☎ *01 42 61 22 37* • *Daily to 10:30 pm* • 🚇 *Rue du Bac*

Good location near the Seine. Since 1919, this has been a classic with reasonable prices, every dish presented *comme il faut*.

LE ROUGE VIF

48, rue de Verneuil • ☎ *01 42 86 81 87* • 🚇 *Rue du Bac*

Monday-Friday to 10 pm, closed Saturday and Sunday

A charming bistro in a former stable; the menu sticks to the middle of the road, but does it well.

8TH ARRONDISSEMENT

✦

CHEZ TANTE LOUISE

41, rue Boissy-d'Anglas • ☎ *01 42 65 06 85* • 🚇 *Madeleine, Concorde*

Monday-Friday to 10:15 pm, closed Saturday and Sunday

A Christmas Eve dinner here (*réveillon*) engraved itself on our hearts forever. With a Burgundian menu, a fine wine list, and attentive service.

L'ECLUSE

15, place de la Madeleine • ☎ *01 42 65 34 69*

Daily to 1 am • 🚇 *Madeleine*

This wine bar specializing in Bordeaux, one of a chain of five around the city, offers a limited bistro menu. Also located at:

• *15, quai des Grands-Augustins, 6th*

• *64, rue François Premier, 8th*

• *13, rue de la Roquette, 11th*

• *1, rue de l'Armaillé, 17th*

9TH ARRONDISSEMENT

✦

ROSE BAKERY

46, rue des Martyrs • ☎ *01 42 82 12 80* • 🚇 *Pigalle, Saint-Georges*

Tuesday-Saturday 9 am to 7 pm; Sunday 10 am to 6 pm; closed Monday

This tiny takeout lunch place has half a dozen small tables, a variety of salads, and a few hot dishes, some with a British twist. Bargain prices for hearty organic food and a pleasant vin de table bring crowds at noon.

10TH ARRONDISSEMENT

✦

LA GRILLE

80, rue du Faubourg-Poissonnière • ☎ *01 47 70 89 73*

Monday-Friday to 9:30 pm, closed Saturday and Sunday

🚇 *Barbès-Rochechouart, Possonière*

An old-fashioned bistro of a type that may be going out of style.

11TH ARRONDISSEMENT

✦

CHARDENOUX

1, rue Jules Vallès • ☎ *01 43 71 49 52*

Daily to 11:30 pm • 🚇 *Charonne*

Come here for wonderful turn-of-the-century decor, a fabulous wine list, and absolutely reliable dishes.

JACQUES MÉLAC

42, rue Léon Frot • ☎ *01 40 09 93 37* • 🚇 *Charonne*

Monday-Saturday to 10:30 pm, closed Sunday

This is simple home cooking, with a wine list full of enchanting discoveries.

12TH ARRONDISSEMENT

✦

A LA BICHE AU BOIS

45, avenue Ledru-Rollin • ☎ *01 43 43 34 38* • 🚇 *Gare de Lyon*

Monday-Friday to 11 pm; closed Saturday, Sunday, and Monday lunch

There's an inclination toward the pretentious with a specialty of wild game, but our meal was superb. It's popular, so make a reservation.

A LA FRÉGATE

30, avenue Ledru-Rollin • ☎ *01 43 43 90 32* • 🚇 *Gare de Lyon*

Monday-Friday to 10 pm; closed Saturday and Sunday

Somewhat dark, but honest food in a pleasant ambience. Seafood recommended.

L'ÉBAUCHOIR

43-45, rue de Citeaux • ☎ *01 23 42 49 31* • 🚇 *Faidherbe-Chaligny*

Monday-Saturday to 11 pm; closed Sunday

Well-prepared food in an unadorned environment; simple, noisy, fast.

L'OULETTE

15, place Lachambaudie • ☎ *01 40 02 02 12* • 🚇 *Dugommier*

Monday-Saturday to 10:15 pm; closed Saturday lunch and Sunday

Pretty little place in a hidden corner of Bercy; the cooking is inventive and satisfying.

LE QUINCY

28, avenue Ledru-Rollin • ☎ 01 46 28 46 76 • 🚇 Gare de Lyon
Monday-Friday to 10:15 pm; closed Saturday and Sunday

Traditional menu, somewhat expensive, but the food and ambience will not disappoint.

LE SQUARE TROUSSEAU

1, rue Antoine Vollon • ☎ 01 43 43 06 00 • 🚇 Ledru Rollin
Tuesday-Saturday to 11:30 pm; closed Sunday and Monday

Traditional bistro fare in an agreeable setting; often full, so reserve.

LE TRAIN BLEU

Gare de Lyon, 20, boulevard Diderot • ☎ 01 43 43 09 06
Daily to 11 pm • 🚇 Gare de Lyon

Above the waiting room you'll find yourself in a magnificent space under a gloriously painted ceiling. Classic brasserie food is not great but reliable, though somewhat expensive.

AU TROU GASCON

40, rue Taine • ☎ 01 43 44 34 26 • 🚇 Daumesnil
Monday-Friday to 10 pm, closed Saturday and Sunday

The cooking of the southwest is at its best here. The wine list is replete with the pick of Bordeaux, and great Armagnac. We love all of it.

LES ZYGOMATES

7, rue de Capri • ☎ *01 40 19 93 04* • 🚇 *Michel Bizot*

Monday-Saturday to 10:15 pm; closed Saturday lunch and Sunday

A former butcher shop, it's noisy and crowded, but the attractive prices may explain why it's hard to get a table.

13TH ARRONDISSEMENT

✦

LE PETIT MARGUERY

9, boulevard de Port-Royal • ☎ *01 43 31 58 59* • 🚇 *Gobelins*

Tuesday-Saturday to 10:15 pm; closed Sunday and Monday

Generous portions and rapid service make this a good stop.

14TH ARRONDISSEMENT

✦

LE BISTRO DU DÔME

1, rue Delambre • ☎ *01 43 35 42 00*

Daily to 11 pm • 🚇 *Edgar-Quinet*

Offshoot of Le Dôme, perhaps less impressive in decor but not as expensive. For fish and shellfish, look no farther.

LE DÔME

108, boulevard du Montparnasse • ☎ *01 43 35 25 81*

Daily to midnight • 🚇 *Vavin*

If you crave seafood properly prepared, this is the place for it, in a beautiful belle epoque brasserie.

15TH ARRONDISSEMENT

✦

L'OSTRÉADE

11, boulevard de Vaugirard • ☎ *01 43 21 87 41*

Daily to 11:15 pm • 🚇 *Montparnasse Bienvenue*

This is a haven for the seafood lover; well-prepared dishes at attractive prices.

16TH ARRONDISSEMENT

✦

LA BUTTE CHAILLOT

110bis, avenue Kléber • ☎ *01 47 27 88 88*

Daily to 11 pm; closed Saturday lunch • 🚇 *Trocadéro*

Busy, classic, but what you expect is served here just as you expect it.

LE CUISINIER FRANÇOIS

19, rue le Marois • ☎ *01 45 27 83 74* • 🚇 *Porte de Saint-Cloud*

Tuesday-Sunday to 10:30 pm; closed Sunday dinner and Monday

Small dining room, modest menu, reasonable prices.

MAISON PRUNIER

16, avenue Victor-Hugo • ☎ *01 44 17 35 85.*

Daily to 1 am; closed Sunday

The dining room evokes what fine dining used to be in art deco Paris. seafood dishes are their strong suit.

17TH ARRONDISSEMENT

✦

LE BALLON DES TERNES

103, avenue des Ternes • ☎ *01 45 74 17 98*

Daily to midnight • 🚇 *Porte Maillot*

A big, busy, brasserie in the classic style, and the food is always reliable; large nonsmoking section.

20TH ARRONDISSEMENT

✦

LES ALLOBROGES

71, rue des Grands-Champs • ☎ *01 43 73 40 00* • 🚇 *Maraîchers*

Tuesday-Saturday to 10 pm; closed Sunday and Monday

Far from central Paris, but the decor is pleasing, the menu is intriguing, and the presentation is appealing.

BIBLIOGRAPHY

Little is written about the markets of Paris. Most of the material in this book we observed directly. Occasionally Le Figaro or the International Herald Tribune will publish something on markets. However, this short list of books may help you pursue particular interests in more depth.

Armstrong, Jack, and Delores Wilson. Boulangerie: *Pocket Guide to Paris's Famous Bakeries.* Ten Speed, 1999.

Ballard, Ginette (ed.). Secrets of Paris: *A Guidebook for the Discerning Traveler.* Thomasson- Grant, 1994.

Bernstein, Michael A. *The Paris Guide: Fourth Edition.* Michael A. Bernstein, April 2004.

Clemente, Maribeth. *The Riches of Paris: A Shopping and Touring Guide.* Griffin Trade Paperback, 2001.

Downie, David. Paris, *Paris.* Transatlantic, 2005.

Drake, Alicia. *A Shopper's Guide to Paris Fashion.* Metro, 2000.

Fierro, Alfred. *Historical Dictionary of Paris.* Scarecrow, 1997.

Gershman, Suzy. *Frommer's Born to Shop: Paris.* IDG Books Worldwide, 2000.

Gopnik, Adam. *Paris to the Moon.* Random House, 2000.

Hamburger, Robert and Barbara. *Bistros of Paris.* Ecco, 2001.

Kaplan, Rachel. *Little-Known Museums In and Around Paris.* Harry N. Abrams, 1996.

Lown, Patricia Twohill, and David Lown. *Tout Paris: The Source Guide to the Art of French Decoration.* Palancar, 1994.

Meyer, Nicolle Aimee, and Amanda Pilar Smith. *Paris in a Basket: Markets—the Food and the People*. Könemann, 2000.

Paris, Mode d'Emploi/User's Guide. Office de Tourism de Paris, n.d.

Thomas, Rupert, and Eglé Salvy. *Antique and Flea Markets of Paris and London*. Thames and Hudson, 1999.

Thomazeau, François, and Sylvain Ageorges. *The Authentic Bistros of Paris*. Little Bookroom, 2005.

Webb, Michael. *Through the Windows of Paris: Fifty Unique Shops*. Balcony, 1999.

Wells, Patricia. *The Food Lover's Guide to Paris, 4th ed.* Workman, 1999.

Williams, Ellen. *The Historic Restaurants of Paris: A Guide to Century-Old Cafés, Bistros, and Gourmet Food Shops*. Little Bookroom, 2001.

Young, Daniel. *Paris Café Cookbook*. William Morrow, 1998.

Zagat Survey, 2005/06: Paris Restaurants. Local editors: Alexander Lobrano, Mary Des champs. Zagat Survey, 2005.

MARKETS INDEX

RESTAURANTS, BISTROS, AND BRASSERIES

About the Authors

Dixon Long and Ruthanne Long are co-authors of *Markets of Provence*. He is also a novelist and short story writer, as well as dean emeritus and professor emeritus of political science at Case Western Reserve University. Ruthanne Long was a food consultant for wineries in the Napa Valley. They have lived in Provence and Paris.